Happier
More
Often

Happier
More Often

A long letter from a friend

HARRY VAN BOMMEL

Resources Supporting Family
and Community Legacies Inc.
Toronto, Ontario 2009

Copyright 1990, 2009, Harry van Bommel
Cover photo: copyright 2009, Harry van Bommel with
thanks to Joanna Klees van Bommel for the cover concept.
Cover and book design by Laura Brady
(www.bradytypesetting.com)

LIBRARY AND ARCHIVES CANADA CATALOGUING IN PUBLICATION
van Bommel, Harry
    Happier more often : a long letter from a friend /
Harry van Bommel.

Includes bibliographical references.
ISBN 978-1-55307-058-0

1. Happiness. I. Resources Supporting Family and Community
Legacies Inc. II. Title.

BJ1481.V35 2007   152.4'2   C2007-906280-6

To contact the author about speaking engagements, write or call:
HARRY VAN BOMMEL
Resources Supporting Family and Community Legacies Inc.
11 Miniot Circle
Toronto, ON M1K 2K1 Canada
(416) 264 4665
harry@legacies.ca www.legacies.ca
www.happiermoreoften.com

To Janet, Joanna and Bram

who let me join in their happiness everyday

Contents

Foreword

IMAGINE YOURSELF waiting for a long letter (say 31,000 words or so long!) from a friend of yours. The person who delivers your mail smiles when she gives you this book. *Looks like a long night of reading!*

I have been known to send pretty long letters to my friends in the past. In some I have written some powerful thoughts (or at least I thought so!). I also felt like there was more to say and that I should put a bit more effort into it, a little more thought.

THIS LITTLE BOOK IS MY LETTER TO YOU. I have organized it into little chunks so that it makes good bathroom, beach, car/bus/train/plane, or just-sit-around-with-a-hot-drink kind of reading. Think of it as one person's ideas right now to a friend. The thoughts are not perfect. My ideas may change (I will keep you informed). Some day you may read the book again and find new things with which to agree and disagree. That's great. Our thoughts and beliefs evolve over time. I am not preaching the gospel according to HvB but rather giving you an excuse to spend some time thinking about your own ideas on happiness, philosophy, etc. Happiness is an ever-evolving kind of work. It is fun too!

What do I know about happiness? Am I a psychologist or a wise man? Just because I have written other books, does that mean I know enough to write about such a big subject as happiness? No to all of the above!

But I am a learner and I am a teacher. We often learn best through preparation to teach others. Writing is a similar process. What I have learned may help you. What you learn from this book will help others you know if you pass along your thoughts. There is nothing new within the study of happiness. The information is all out there. I have just tried to condense some of it for your practical, day-to-day use.

Like you, I have my ups and downs. I wanted to figure out ways to have more of the ups, even if they last only a few seconds or minutes during particularly difficult moments in my life. I wanted to find ways to help me cope with the inevitable daily frustrations so that I could look beyond the moment to remember that I do control more of my emotions than I often credit myself.

I'm not the poster boy for being happy all the time. There are times when I feel profoundly unhappy, like when my parents died, when my first business failed, when relationships ended, or when I say good-bye to people at airports or train stations whom I love and may never see again.

This book is to remind us that we all have ways to increase the amount of time we are happy. Being happier in the present is so much easier to control than planning to be happy in the future when we accomplish something important, buy something we have always wanted, earn enough money to be happy, or find our soul mate.

Perhaps some of what I have learned through experience or through the experiences of others can help you feel more in control of your thoughts and feelings as well so that you have more moments of happiness too. Everything you learn and have learned, I hope you pass along to others. Together we can all get better at choosing to be happier more often.

So here is my long letter to you. I hope you find it helpful.

Happily (more often than I used to be anyway!) and gratefully yours,

HARRY
Toronto, Canada
August 30, 2009

Introduction

WILLIAM JAMES said that happiness is the secret motive that drives everyone. I do not know if that is true because our motivations come from various sources including family history, pride, greed, love, and environmental pressures. I think James is right, however, that the consequences of our motives, personally, often have their route in *wanting to feel good* or *contented*. People can feel good cheating, lying and being violent when these actions achieve some of their personal goals. Their happiness is not what most of us would call *good* happiness — but it is happiness for them nonetheless.

This book is about the positive forms of happiness that lead people to *do good* while *feeling good*. The book was originally a long letter I wrote when I was 35 years old and gave to various friends and colleagues as a gift. I asked them for suggestions on how to improve the letter to make it more helpful for others. Then I put the letter aside and lived another 19 years!

Nineteen years is not a long time in history but it is a big chunk of my adult life. A person I had not seen in many years told me that my original letter had helped her through a difficult divorce. I was touched by her thoughtfulness in letting me know that my letter had helped her. I dusted off the original letter and read it again with much fresher eyes. Since my 35th birthday, my wife and I have had two wonderful children, have moved into our first (and probably last!) house, changed our jobs to self-employment, and began home schooling our children — which has been a great source of happiness for all of us.

Have my thoughts from the age of 35 stood the test of time—at least the test of a relatively short time? They have, I'm pleased to say. My views years ago are quite consistent with my views now, only I have more experiences and stories to tell. There are some universal truths and they have helped me through some difficult times in the past decades as they had in my early years. Perhaps some of these truths will help you too.

~

The word *happiness*, like the word *love*, is often used to mean too many things to many people. The definition of *happiness* could be:

- characterized by good fortune; prosperous; having or demonstrating pleasure; gratified.
- experiencing joy, pleasure and bliss.
- having, showing or causing a feeling of great pleasure, joy, contentment, satisfaction.
- a sense of subjective well-being.
- the capacity to enjoy life.

Few people can tell you what happiness is yet most of us know when we are happy. We are often happy when a child trusts us to hold their hand as we cross the street. We are happy to see someone we love accomplish something they set out to do. We are often happy when a best friend remembers to thank us for being who we are. We are often happy when we feel needed, valued, loved and liked.

I do not know how to define happiness any better than that—knowing that we are needed, valued, loved and liked yet understanding that happiness is something we give ourselves. Like dignity, persistence, pride and honor, happiness is something inside us that we control more often than not.

Can you be happy all the time? Do you want to be happy all the time? Do you need long periods of suffering, guilt and unhappiness to benefit fully from being happy? How is happiness different from having fun, or laughing or feeling peaceful or feeling contented or satisfied? What makes you happy? What makes you unhappy? Can anything MAKE you happy or sad?

Lots of questions....maybe this little book will help you find a few of your own answers. The purpose of this book (or very long letter!) is very simple: to help all of us choose to be happy more often than we are now. That is it. Nothing too fancy. Not happy all the time. Just to be happy more often than we are now. I wrote the book because I have been able to choose to be happier a little more often than I used to. Like all writers I hope that some of my experiences can help other people. Writing also makes choosing to be happy more real to me. It is hard to write down your thoughts and not try to practice what you have *preached* to others! You can do the same for your family and friends!

If this book helps you feel happy just a bit more than you are now, then I hope you will pass on that happiness to others–a smile will do. Remember what I say is not what is important in this book. There are no unique ideas anymore about happiness. But you are unique, so your approach to life will be your own. Find things that are useful in this book and pass them on to others. Remind yourself of what helps your happiness now and do more of it.

Much of my own writing is in the field of caregiving, hospice palliative care and grieving. My work with people who are dying constantly reminds me that what we tend to regret most not having spent enough time with the people we love most doing the things we love to do. We have spent too much doing things we do not love and doing it with people whose names we cannot even remember any more. Make changes now so you don't have those regrets.

One last little suggestion—feel free to mark up the book any time an inspiration strikes you. Use the margins or the top and bottom of the pages to write down any thoughts that you would like to remember. If you should read this book again in 10 years, you will be able to see how your thoughts and beliefs have stayed the same and how some have evolved into a wiser way to enjoy the life you have.

If you like what you are learning, pass the book on to others. Remember that younger people in your life could benefit from this book just as older people and everyone in between. Everyone can choose to be happier more often starting today.

Why Being Unhappy Is Easier

WHY ARE SO many people unhappy so much of the time? Because it is easier and expected!

There are 10 rules we are conditioned to follow to succeed. These are unwritten rules because they go against what we learned from our parents and teachers at a young age when we were supposed to learn the ideals of good living.

The presumption is, that if you follow these 10 rules you will succeed personally, professionally and financially. There is a presumption that these things will make you happy and fulfill an immediate gratification—even if you will likely not be happier in the long run.

Being unhappy is easier. There are thousands of books, videos and audio tapes and courses on how to be happy, successful or at peace. Yet many people choose to be unhappy much of the time.

Don't believe me? Walk into a room full of strangers and watch how people strike up a conversation. You will find that most start with a complaint: *The weather really sucks today, right? Can you believe those politicians? Who hired that guy to play for our team anyway? He's not worth the money!* If you entered that room all happy and full of energy, most people would be suspicious–some might even think you are on drugs!

So it's easier to follow some of the unofficial rules of success below. These are the ones that society teaches us through media, work relationships, and economics are good rules to follow. We learn and practice them consciously or unconsciously to be successful. Living this way is comfortable. Living this way is more predictable and easier. Living this way fits in better with people around us.

Sadly, in the long run, they also usually lead us feeling unfulfilled. Then we pick up the next book, DVD or seminar on how to find happiness again.

Do you practice any of these rules now?

SOCIETY'S 10 RULES FOR BEING SUCCESSFUL (AND UNHAPPY)

1. Lie – it's easier – but don't get caught.
2. Cheat – you'll get ahead faster – but, again, don't get caught.
3. Steal – people expect it anyway – but, you guessed it, don't get caught.
4. Abuse power – what else is it for.
5. Abuse love – you can always get more.
6. Abuse your body with drugs, alcohol, tobacco, food and certainly no exercize – you only live once.
7. Abuse your mind – watch more TV and sports – you can avoid being overwhelmed by real life this way.
8. Abuse your soul – value and trust only yourself.

9. Complain and critique everything – always see the glass as half empty because, damn it, it is.

10. Hoard as much money and things as you can – it's how the world keeps score of who is winning.

Remember; if you have moments of happiness – don't worry – they always go away. Life is hard. No one will do you any favors. Get what you can when you can. You only live once. If you follow any of these rules, regularly, you will come to a place in your life when you ask, *Is that all there is?* Some people call it a mid-life crisis. Others call it a longing for something more. Some call it a spiritual crisis. Others, a sense of being lost and alone.

Do you want something better? Are you satisfied with where your life has led you? If you measure how often a day you are happy, is it enough?

Is where you work a place of enjoyment, productivity, laughter and life-long friendship?

Do you want it to be? If you spend 8-10 hours of each day working, wouldn't you like to go home more often energized with news to tell your loved ones about what a great day you had?

If you answer yes to any of these questions, then follow the rules in the next section to be happier more often.

10 Rules for being Happier More Often

(and Successful!)

You've read what society teaches us (unofficially of course) what the real life rules of success look like. Here are the rules that a combination of a wise soul, an elder and a young child might give you. I'm going to start from the bottom of the list and move to the #1 rule you can do to be happier more often.

10. SMILE and laugh more often. A 10-minute belly laugh massages your internal organs better than hours of quiet meditation.

9. BREATHE slowly and deeply at least 3 times a day for 5-10 minutes. You can do this while you are working at your desk, driving your car, walking your dog, waiting in a line, etc.

8. MUSIC — listen, sing, write, or dance. Use energizing or relaxing music, depending on how you would like to be happy at that moment.

7. RELATIONSHIPS — nurture the ones you have; create new ones with people older and younger. If you work 10-12 hour days and say you are doing it for your family, you are kidding yourself. Absence does not make the heart grow founder if you are absent most of every day of your working life. Go home and nurture your family and friends.

6. EMOTIONAL JOY — find out what makes you smile, laugh, and feel peaceful and write down your favorite 10. Then do them more often. It could be watching your child sleep, sitting quietly on a park bench, watching a favorite comedy on TV, going for lunch or a walk with a dear friend you rarely see, sharing a family meal together more often, holding hands with your sweetie, eating some of Mom's homemade

cookies or working with your Dad on a project. Whatever works for you, do it more often. Don't wait for retirement or for when you have more time.

5. INTELLECTUAL INTERESTS – knowledge is power and power gives one a sense of confidence and happiness. Find out about what you need to know to live a good life, as you define it. Learn about managing your finances instead of letting money manage you. Find out about what you need to do to stay healthy. How will you provide care to your parents, spouse, children, friends, neighbors? Learn these things as you need them and teach others when they need the same knowledge and skills. *Always look for the wonder in learning and teach what you learn to others. Inspire others through your experiences.*

4. PHYSICALLY MOVE around to release natural endorphins that make you feel good and to act as distractions. Even if you are stuck in one place, find ways to move your body and at your earliest chance, move it in a dif-

ferent place (e.g., home, forest, beach, playground) to benefit from the change of scene as well.

3. PRACTICE A LIFE-AFFIRMING BELIEF beyond yourself. Whether through religion, a more general spirituality or a love of nature, go beyond yourself so you have something to hold on to when you need that strength, courage, and persistence. Belief only in yourself or your family and friends may mean you do not have the resources to struggle through really difficult times nor the comfort of feeling part of something bigger and better.

2. APPLY ANCIENT WISDOM – We are not alone. We are not the first people to try and figure out the meaning of life or how to live a good life. Learn what other people have concluded after lifetimes of study and experiences. We have so much more in common with people of different cultures and from different centuries.

1. HAPPIERMOREOFTEN NOW – Put the other 9 rules to work starting now. Return to them often. Go to our website for further ideas, tips, reports on studies and to share your experiences with others. When you reverse the order of the rules above you will get a *HAPPIER MBS*. This is a tongue-in-cheek way of saying there is so much BS in the world, find the true gems of how to enjoy your life everyday; more often, than you do now. When you do, you will be happier more often and have earned a *Masters in Being Successful* (MBS)! Congratulations!

H appier more often

A pply ancient wisdom

P ractice a life-affirming belief

P hysically move

I ntellectual interests

E motional joy

R elationships – nurture and create new ones

M usic

B reathe slowly and deeply

S mile and laugh more often!

It's OK to be
Mad, Bad and Sad
Sometimes

Let's get this one out of the way right now. All of us get mad sometimes. All of us behave badly sometimes. All of us experience sadness and so many other emotions throughout our life. Mark Twain once wrote that the worst person in the world to live is someone who is a good example. No one wants to live with a saint because you can never attain that level of perfection. That doesn't mean you cannot, or should not, strive to improve yourself. It just means that you recognize that none of us is perfect, all of us are mad, bad and sad sometimes and that life does not stop when we behave in these ways.

Since you and I are not perfect, we have lots of room to improve! We can get mad less often about things that in the greater scheme of things don't matter. The book *Don't Sweat the Small Stuff...and It's All Small Stuff* may be a helpful guide for you.

We all do things that someone else might consider bad. We may overeat, drink too much, or do not usually practice good nutrition or physical exercize. Sometimes we hurt others intentionally because we think they have deserved it. More often we hurt people unintentionally and they rarely tell us what we have done so we live blissfully on without knowing the hurt we have caused.

In science it is sometimes the case that an exception to a rule nullifies the rule and requires a completely new rule. The same is not true about happiness. If you are mad, bad or sad sometimes it does not rule out the possibility that you will be happy again. We can no more be happy 100% of the time than we can be sad or mad 100% of the time. *This whole book is about changing the odds slightly or mightily in favor of being happier more often. That's it. Not rocket science. Just being happier more often than now.*

Your Own Top 10 Strategies for Being Successful and Happier More Often

What are your rules? Think about that for a moment. Jot down some points below. You can add to this list as you go through the book. When you are comfortable with your list, follow your own rules. When you do, it is easier to make life-defining decisions. It is easier to choose between earning more money or spending more time with family and friends. It makes it easier to decide how to live your life, day-to-day.

1.

2.

3.

4.

5.

6.

7.

8.

9.

_____

_____

10.

_____

_____

DON'T FORGET: This book is about giving you, not society, control over what makes you happy…more often. This book is about you and for you. Take what is helpful and, for now, ignore the rest. Then share what you have learned because one of the wisest learnings through the centuries is that sharing your happiness increases your own.

Happiness, Fun and Peacefulness

HAPPINESS AND FUN

Fun is what we experience when we are doing something. It makes the rest of the world go away for a while and gives us something else to concentrate on. Like watching television, going to an amusement park or zoo, getting dressed up for a glamorous party, or playing or watching sports. Some people use things like alcohol and drugs to have fun. Some people jog for miles, read books, or write long philosophic letters to friends to have fun.

HAPPINESS IS AN ATTITUDE OF LIVING. We can choose to be happy before, during and after doing something. Happiness is a way of thinking and a way of living. It is deeper in emotions and lasts longer. If you feel good about your-self, about your personal and working life, then you are probably happy. If you are happy and are having fun too then you get the bonus of creating memories that will help you in years to come when you may have less time for fun.

HAPPINESS AND PEACEFULNESS

Is there a difference between someone who has found happiness and someone who has found a sense of peacefulness in their lives?

Happiness and peacefulness are similar. Watching a child sleep may help you feel both happy and peaceful. Watching that same child perform on the balance beam in gymnastic with genuine joy may also help you feel happy but you may not feel very peaceful until they dismount safely!

These concepts can be difficult to describe in words. What is more obvious is that our eyes, our face, our body language and our actions will tell the people around us how we feel no matter what words we use to describe it. That is the beauty of happiness, peacefulness, joy, wonder, love, calmness and excitement—people know when we feel this way long before we tell them.

Happiness Day-to-Day

Each day is a new opportunity to find ways to become happier and share that happiness with others.

Does that sound corny or what! Yet, how often do you remember someone holding a door for you, sharing a bright *Good morning!* or offering to let you move ahead of them in the grocery line since you have so few things to buy? How often has someone offered you one of their candies or sent you a funny email to brighten your day? How often do people just smile when they see you coming? Whether you get these things a lot or not, the point is you can increase any of these things by being happier, more often, yourself. Happiness breeds happiness just as a room full of complaining, whining people tends to breed more of the same. You can be the catalyst that changes peoples' lives for that moment. You can.

There are also daily opportunities to observe our surroundings and thrive on the beauty around us. For example, on one visit to my family in Europe I took a train from my sister's home in Germany to my aunt's home in The Netherlands. I love train trips because they are a perfect time for me to think about my past, present and future. So many things that you see during a train trip remind you of things you might otherwise forget.

On this particular trip along the Rhine River I saw castles, vineyards, and endless water. All of these things have been changed by time, people, pollution and history but there were still timeless elements to it all. The green mountain sides, the visions of wasteful wars, the white castle with pink brick trim sitting on a small island in the middle of the Rhine, and the Loreley Mountain made famous by poetry and songs. There was even a freighter ship with the same name as my mother, *Koos*. Remembering my mother brought back other members of her and our times together. All of these observations encouraged me to write furiously on odd pieces of paper thoughts that I knew I might want to use in this book.

Remembering something that worked for us in the past can encourage us to do it more often now. If I were to ask you about important things that happened in your life this past month, what would you answer? Let me give you a few examples of how lucky I am.

For example in one month: my wife baked some goodies and encouraged me to test EVERYTHING, two friends decorated an Elvis bust with Christmas lights in my office, a person took my picture as a memory of our working together, my aunt called from Europe just to tell me she missed me, a friend of mine wrote her autobiography and allowed me to help, a bus driver smiled broadly and wished me a good morning, a student told me that my class helped him see his life differently, another student said I wrote in a way that helped her learn, and three special secretaries I worked with saved jokes for me and helped me smile on difficult days, the cashier in a cafeteria said she missed seeing me, a waitress gave me an extra bun with my salad, my colleagues literally applauded when I finished a long assignment, one of my clients told me there was a waiting list for my course, I was asked to speak at four different special events, and so on, and so on.

What wonderful memories these people knowingly, and unknowingly, gave me. Some were planned out while others just happened. *These are regular people giving gifts of memory to another regular person on a day-to-day basis.* There is no evil intention present. There is no expectation of a returned favor. Just people being good for goodness sake.

By remembering some of the wonderful things that happened to me encouraged me to do some of these things for others.

When I pray each night before falling asleep I go over my day and remember all the good things that happened to me that day. Some days are filled with more happiness than others. When a day is particularly hard or troublesome I borrow memories from other days and feel grateful to have lived another day. Gratitude in prayer is a wonderful sleeping pill. It rests the mind (usually) and relaxes the body. *Even when my worries overwhelm my gratitude it takes only a day or two to remember how lucky I am.*

Would it not be nice to live a bit of our lives as if we were in a sentimental movie? People laugh and cry at corny movies like *It's a Wonderful Life* or *Miracle on 34th Street* for a reason. We are reminded of how small kindnesses can influence lives for decades. We learn that thoughtfulness of one person may come to them years later when they need support most.

If we acted as if we were living in a sentimental movie we would likely give flowers to people for no particular reason. We would sing in the rain more often. We would prepare a lovely dinner for our family or friends in the middle of the week when they did not expect it or maybe make a special date with a loved one so they could join in the fun of something special. We would call people we have not talked to in years just to say hello. We would hold doors open for women and men. We would say *please* and *thank you* more often. We would judge people less and build their confidence more. We would be thoughtful to those in grief. We would help correct a person's mistake without making them feel badly. We would offer our help without an expectation of having it returned. We would be more respectful of older people and not call them honey or sweetie unless they asked us to. We would help others without getting a tax receipt for it. We would strive toward more happy endings. We would smile more when we looked at ourselves in a mirror. We would be a bit happier than we are right now.

When Happiness Does Not Work

I have said from the beginning that we probably cannot be happy all the time. I may be trying to be happy more often than not, but I am enough of a realist to know that it is not always possible for different reasons. I am inherently a moody person. I understand that what I am writing about takes thoughtful, conscientious, ongoing effort. It is worth that effort but sometimes lying in bed longer and hiding under the covers is easier — and dare I say it — even feels better!

For example, it may seem hard to be happy if you have not had enough sleep, have not been eating well or, in extreme circumstances, have no place to live. People would not expect you to be happy in these situations...yet some people are happy in similar circumstances for some of the time.

When we look at people who have survived extreme cases of torture, degradation, or isolation we find that many of them still write or talk about being happy. They have faced the worst possible conditions and are still able to talk about being happy.

When we look at people who have grown up in poor areas of world, who have suffered humiliation, lack of education or proper nutrition we still find that they talk about happiness. They talk about the love of their family, the encouragement of their friends, the guidance of their teachers and their faith in something beyond their control. They talk about moments of genuine happiness in situations where we cannot imagine ourselves finding any happiness.

Perhaps one of the best known survivors of the concentration camps in World War II is Viktor E. Frankl. Dr. Frankl was a famous psychiatrist who lived through the horrors of several death camps. In his book, *Man's Search for Meaning*, Dr. Frankl gives some wonderful examples of how he suffered the loss of all of his family, including watching his wife taken away to her death. In his practice he sometimes asks his patients who suffer from all sorts of problems, large and small, *Why do you not commit suicide?* In asking people this ultimate question he learns that people want to live for many reasons. Through his question they find out what they are living for and perhaps how they can live more fully.

Dr. Frankl's most profound, personal conclusion was that: *We who lived in concentration camps can remember the men who walked through the huts comforting others, giving away their last piece of bread. They have been few in number, but they offer sufficient proof that everything can be taken from a man but one thing:* **the last of the human freedoms — to choose one's attitude in any given set of circumstances, to choose one's own way.** [emphasis added]

He goes on to talk about the daily choices

one has, in any situation. The choice to reach out to help someone else or to ask for help. The opportunity to recognize the humanity in someone regardless of the circumstances. The ability to remember the people we love and who love us so that we have a reason to fight to live another day. The ability to foresee a future where one's dreams can still be partially fulfilled.

For Dr. Frankl, one of his images of himself was in the future teaching at the university where he had been a professor and talking to his students about how to survive a holocaust. He imagined the hell he was experiencing as a lesson for his students.

When my parents were dying, I saw myself in the future teaching others how to care for their loved ones at home more competently than I was able to do myself at the time. I wanted my 'hell' to lead to helping others find more genuine moments of happiness with their loved ones in similar circumstances. This image of myself helped me enormously in some of the most difficult days of my life.

We can learn from people who have suffered situations we only have nightmares about. They still talk about being happy. They all seem to be telling us that happiness is not something you feel once everything else is okay in your life. You do not need to wait to have financial security. You do not have to wait until you have found the perfect mate. You do not have to wait until your children grow up and become happy themselves. You do not have to wait until the cows come home (I could not resist!). Happiness, or at the very least, a bit of happiness is inside of you whenever you want it.

One of the reasons we stop ourselves from being happy may surprise you. Some of us are are afraid to be happy. Some of us, including me on occasion, think we need to be sad, afraid, guilty or suffer to serve a purpose. We may have these feelings because that is what we think 'normal' people feel in similar situations. We may feel that these feelings will bring our family and friends closer to us. We may feel that we do not deserve to be happy because we think happy people have earned their happiness. Or we may think the reverse—that happy people are not 'realists' and that their happiness is only an illusion.

The question for those of us who believe that unhappiness is necessary in order to accomplish things (e.g., being unhappy about how we look will force us to lose weight?) should ask if we can accomplish those same things and be happy as well. For example, can we call someone we have not talked to for a long time without having to feel guilty first? Can we help people who have suffered a hurricane or a flood or a major fire without feeling we have to. Can we miss someone who died years ago without feeling sad that they are no longer with us? Can we be happy when we are around someone we dislike or do we need to acknowledge our dislike for the person by being unhappy? Can we be happy while awaiting surgery or must we overwhelm ourselves with worry to prove to ourselves that it is serious? Must we dislike the partner we divorce to justify the end of a relationship?

What does being sad do for us? What does anger do for us? What does hatred do for us? What would happen if we were not sad, angry or hateful? Could we still achieve what we want? Of course we could.

Here are some other reasons people choose to be unhappy more often than they choose to be happy. Do any of these ideas ring any bells for you?

It's not fair that people cheat, steal, hurt others etc. and get away with it. Question: Does one need to be angry or unhappy about that unfairness to make it different?

I'm not satisfied yet. There is so much left for me to do and accomplish. Questions: What is your definition of satisfaction? Can you ever reach satisfaction based on your definition? Is satisfaction based on getting what you want or working toward getting things so that the journey never ends?

When I used to teach self-defense to people of all ages I was always amazed at how people would judge the possible success of the particular method of self-defense I was teaching. What I was teaching would help people in just about all forms of violent situations imaginable. However it could not help people who were attacked by surprise (e.g., clubbed from behind) or people who were the targets of trained assassins. For some people that was proof positive that the methods were not successful at all.

When I mentioned that someone shot President Reagan with all the secret service people around him or that people cannot possibly defend themselves without knowing that they were under attack they began to get more realistic.

One student in particular was fun to listen to. He was a young high school student who had studied some martial arts. I had asked for questions from the audience and he asked me what I would do if I was attacked from behind by surprise and the attacker hit me over the head with a brick. He said I would fall face down onto the pavement and this attacker would sit on my back and pound my face into the pavement. *What would you do Mr. van Bommel?*

I could see in the workshop participants that this young student had come up with a situation that frightened them. They looked certain that there was no possible way for me to answer this question. I looked them straight in the eyes and replied, *I would wait till it was over just as I would have to wait if a Mack truck accidentally ran over me.* The audience laughed loudly and understood that no method of self-defense could save you from all forms of violence, but the more self-defense you know, the less likely you are to have to use it.

Like this little story, happiness is not something that overcomes all emotions or solves all problems. There will be situations when you will continue to choose to feel the COMFORT of sadness, anger, and fear. In our lifetimes we have found comfort in having a good cry, being afraid of failure, being sad when we say good-bye to someone at the airport or getting angry at an injustice. The only difference now is that you may begin to see them as choices you make for whatever reasons you have and that you can change those choices if you want to.

Although we have control over how we react to things it will not always feel like it is working in both your mind and heart, just as self-defense does not always work. With practice and success you may choose to be happier more often than you are right now. Feelings of sadness, anger, fear, hate, or unhappiness may still feel necessary during your lifetime. I feel these feelings as all of us do. I am only beginning to recognize, though, that I control the feelings; not some outside person, place or thing chooses how I should feel. I also now realize that even as I feel these emotions, I can choose to shorten the time that I feel them.

I began this book in the belief that all of us can increase the amount of time we are happy. Even increasing our happiness a little bit will help us, and help those around us, to enjoy living this life a little more fully. Having spent some months rewriting the book and getting feedback from people I trust, I continue to believe that humans have an enormous capacity to find ways to increase their happiness and the happiness of people around them. There is no personal, genetic limit to happiness. I don't know how close we can come to being happy, contented, satisfied, at peace and fulfilled in one life-time but I know most of us, including me, has not reached our potential…yet!

*Happiness and
Wisdom*

WISE IN OUR TIME

Do you really have to be 60, 70, 80 or 90 years
old to learn the lessons of life that give wisdom
to some of our older and younger relatives and
acquaintances? Can we not learn the lessons
now so we have more time to enjoy them?

In some cultures people listen to their
older relatives and leaders to find out about
life and about living that life fully. You can read
their stories in the thousands of books written
since people began to write. *You can also learn
from the older, and younger, people in your own life.*
Children and older relatives are not perfect.
They can be cranky, rude and insensitive.
However, *they also live at the two extreme ends of*

life and can help us put the middle years into a different perspective. They can learn from us as we learn from them.

My grandfather was a kindred spirit with me. We did not agree on politics, foreign aid, education, business or religion. We did agree on family, however. He told me that it took him over 75 years to understand the importance of family.

My grandfather had a devoted, strong-minded wife. They had 10 children. He ruled with an iron fist and occasionally a log from the fireplace. Most of his children feared him and some competed with him to see who had the stronger will. By modern standards he would be considered authoritarian, a local farm boy turned wealthy town leader – a respected member of his community but feared at home.

I asked him when he was 91 why he had been so cruel to his own children. He was angry at first at such a rude question from a young grandson. However, he saw my genuine curiosity rather than a judgmental attitude.

After a few minutes of quiet thought, he chose to tell me.

When he was a little boy in the 1890s of the Netherlands he was the youngest son of a farmer. They lived in a small farming community near the local castle owner for whom my great-grandfather worked. My great-grandfather died when my grandfather was only 17 years old. The last thing my grandfather remembered of his father influenced him for the rest of his life. My great-grandfather was lying on his deathbed while my grandfather was standing in the corner of his parents' bedroom. My grandfather, a shy, reserved boy with flaming red hair saw that his strong, authoritarian father was dying. That young man boy was afraid and he was trying to hide into the woodwork of that bedroom wall. His father looked at him and said to his wife, *That boy will never amount to anything.* He was referring to my grandfather having his hands in his pockets—a clear sign at the turn-of-the-century that you were lazy.

My grandfather tried to prove his father wrong for the rest of his life. He built up a successful concrete factory only to see it destroyed during the war. At the age of 56 he started all over again and succeeded. This was a testament to his persistence and his need to succeed.

His role models of how to discipline children were, as he explained it to me, his father, the town's fire-and-brimstone priest, and the head master at his elementary school (a don't-spare-the-rod kind of teacher). The head master had beaten my grandfather's oldest brother to death, literally. The boy was only six years old. As sad as the family must have been at the death of their first born child, it was assumed that the boy must have deserved the punishment even if it had gone too far. The head master received no disciplinary action for his behavior.

My grandfather told me that he raised his children based on these role models. When he was in his late 70s and saw the destructiveness of that discipline plus the effects of having put his business ahead of his family, he personally went to each of his 9 remaining children and apologized. He even flew to Canada (he was scared to death of flying) to apologize to his daughter, my mother. Unfortunately many of his children were in those middle years where their concentration was on other matters and they were not able to take the opportunity to learn from their 'new' father—that was left up to some of the grandchildren.

When he was dying, my grandfather told me some of what he had learned in life. He was sorry for the hurt he had caused people. He was sorry that his religion gave him more fear than comfort. He was glad that some of his grandchildren liked to listen to his advice. He wished his children could accept their own children with his same high expectations but with greater acceptance of their individuality. He wished his family would not fight over his property. He wished people would recognize that the value of family grows over time, not decreases. He wished people would learn from his mistakes and his successes. He wished us more joy and happiness.

CHILDLIKE WONDER

Children, like adults, can be joyful and playful but also spiteful and hurtful. In their first few months, however, they look for wonder and learning in the objects in their crib, in the people who make funny faces at them and talk in such animated voices, in their own bodies and the substances that come from that body. They have not learned to judge good and bad yet. Those are the children I want to talk about.

One of the best philosophic summaries I have read about living life fully and joyfully comes from Robert Fulghum, an American who has been a bartender, folk singer, cowboy, sale representative and a minister. He wrote a short book titled *All I Really Need to Know I Learned in Kindergarten*. The quote below from the book may sound simplistic, even trite. However, really look at the meaning behind the words and find the common wisdom reflected in many of the world ancient religions. His perspective learned in Kindergarten is:

Share everything. Play fair. Don't hit people. Put things back where you found them. Clean up your own mess. Don't take things that aren't yours. Say you're sorry when you hurt somebody. Wash your hands before you eat. Flush. Warm cookies and cold milk are good for you. Live a balanced life — learn some and think some and draw and paint and sing and dance and play and work everyday some. Take a nap every afternoon. When you go out into the world, watch out for traffic, hold hands and stick together. Be aware of wonder.

Some people argue that this 'cute' little saying is too simple for living in the real world . . . that life is harder than that. They believe that some people do greater harm than good in life and must be treated accordingly. They say that life is not a Kindergarten class. We need to grow up and face the world honestly.

To those people, I suggest they visit a kindergarten or visit a playground where young children play. Watch some of them play excitedly and co-operatively with shared toys, games and ideas. Watch some of the others who fight over toys, who fight over who is better and stronger or better looking. Is it really very different from how some adults work and play with each other? Is it really that different from how countries work and play with each other? Is it really that different from how you sometimes work and play with your family, friends and the people you work with?

When you look for the wonder in people, places and things you change how you are looking at 'the real world'. There is evil in this world. There are people who do evil. But we each do something to change a small part of that 'real world.' We can do something to help someone else look for wonder. We can learn from our elders and from our youngest family members. We can create more wonder-filled experiences. We can lead the way in our families and between our friends.

Happiness and Philosophy

Sometimes over lunch with friends, at a cottage or in a letter I get philosophical about life, love and our purpose on earth. I am by no means a disciplined philosopher. My little reading of philosophy tells me that our generation is not the first, nor the last, to ask questions about happiness or the meaning of life. The pursuit of happiness is timeless. It is part of the constitution of some countries. At the same time it was not indexed in the Psychological Abstracts International until 1973 so it has not received the interests of scientific, psychological, and medical experts until recently.

Some people say that I am not a philosopher and so I do not know what I am talking about. They tell me that in the 'real world' ancient and modern philosophers recognized the need for people to be unhappy and happy. This range of emotions is assumed to be necessary because we all seem to experience all of them at some point in our lives. They recognized that evil exists in the world and in the actions of people. They tell me to read philosophy and recognize that life is a complex, difficult thing that requires lots of thought before we go around making life too simple.

I have read some philosophy and am 'happy' to report that no one has it 'right' so far. You see, philosophy, like the definition of love, has so many theories and beliefs that no one alive on earth can ever tell us what is right or wrong, good or bad for all of us. We have had great thinkers who have helped us make decisions about morals and ethics but these ideas have changed over time. For example, at differing times in our history capital punishment was legal for anyone who killed someone else, then only for a selected list of murders (e..g, those who killed police officers and prison guards) and then illegal in some areas of the world but not all. Some of what we believe today is not the same as what people believed thousands of years ago. Some of what we will believe tomorrow will be different from today.

Some people argue that we must have absolute rules of moral actions. Harry S. Truman said (as have many others) that there's nothing new in human nature. *The only thing that changes are the names we give things.... The only thing new in the world is the history you don't know.*

I believe that there are some ultimate truths about how we should behave with each other. I do not believe that in my lifetime the world's population (or even its leadership) will agree on what these truths are.

Since I do not know what all the ultimate truths are I will have to base my decisions of how I act on my beliefs. I think that many of my beliefs are 'right' and that they will remain the same for most of my life. I also think that some of my beliefs will change over my lifetime as I learn from the wisdom of other people and from new experiences I have. A friend of mine told me that the world, like any living thing, must have a birth and a death. I think that we should not let the possibility, or the probability, of a dying world prevent us from making our world, in our generation, a better one.

Some Personal Conclusions

What I have concluded so far is that:

1. How I present happiness and our ability to choose to be happy can be seen as a simple solution to a very complex problem – simple in that it represents a fundamental philosophy upon which most of my actions are based. It can be seen as a philosophy of care, service and devotion to improve whatever part of the world we are able to improve. All philosophies have been proven to benefit some people and to harm others, whether consciously or unconsciously. Since I am not a great world leader I can only influence small parts of my world. Until I have a better way shown to me I have decided to do what I can, to the best of my ability, to live

to the standards of 'above all, do no harm' and when possible do something good. Good, for me, is simply defined as trying to improve myself, my skills and abilities to help others to do the same. If I do this in the spirit of being happy and remaining happy then I have done the most good in the limited time given me on earth.

2. Based on the philosophies I have listened to and read, as well as my own experiences, I have concluded that the ultimate truths are not universally perceived. There are many world views and ancient faiths. They have many things in common but are not universally the same. The best we can accomplish on earth is to take what we assume to be the ultimate truth about what a good life is and how we should behave in a good way toward others (our philosophy) and try to live that philosophy (our actions) consistent with the morals that come from that philosophy.

3. I believe life is basically simple. We have a short time on this earth. Each of us cannot

possibly deal with all the complexities of our interdependent beliefs, cultures and actions. Money is not the way to keep score of how successful or happy you are. When you believe that, life is actually more simple.

We can be thoughtful about what we believe in and what the consequences of those beliefs might be. In order to live successfully we must find a short statement of purpose for ourselves by which we measure our decisions and actions. For me, after long searching and revising, I have chosen the sum of what many world religions suggest is our purpose: *Love God, love others and do not forget to love yourself.* I add to that what Georges Vanier (Governor General of Canada in the early 1960s and my first Canadian hero as a young immigrant here) said, *Look to find how you may serve.*

I have taken these thoughts and created a prayer that includes my statement of beliefs which I then try to use in making day-to-day and longer-term decisions. Although I am not a religious person, I am a prayerful one. Perhaps this prayer will encourage you to write you own prayer with your own set of ultimate beliefs.

Through you, God, we love.
I believe that you are compassionate and are with us always and in all ways.
You taught us to love you, love others and not to forget to love ourselves.
I believe that because of the free will you gave us, we must live with the helpful and harmful consequences of our interconnected decisions and behaviors, both conscious and unconscious.
I am saddened that it is easier to do evil than to do good yet strengthened through my faith that to do good is our primary purpose: for ourselves and with our families, our communities and in the world.
I believe that through individual and collective faiths and actions we can make a positive difference in the lives of others.

Please God, help me keep my faith simple, my
   actions morally coherent and my love genuine
   and abundant.

Does this statement of beliefs lead to happiness? No. The statement reflects those highest order principles by which I try to live. It reflects those beliefs that have made me happy in the past and, therefore, are a summary of what for me I must do to continue to experience happiness, peacefulness, bliss, joy, calmness and excitement. Even, or especially, in periods of difficulties these beliefs give me a direction. I may not always be happy with the direction (cheating, stealing, hoarding are easier after all). Doing 'the right thing' does make me ultimately happy with my choices.

Whenever in doubt with what to do next, find ways to help others. In helping others we fulfil the promise that 'through individual and collective faiths and actions we can make a positive difference in the lives of others.' As long as we live, we have that opportunity to serve others which leads, for many of us, to short and longer-term happiness.

I distil that prayer into an even shorter personal motto:

My happiness comes from living a balanced life of love, gratitude and service.

Happiness and Abuse

When you read the title of this section, you may say to yourself: *Please don't tell us that there is any happiness in being abused as a child or an adult. Please don't try to sugar coat the agony, trauma, devastation that comes from violence either physical or emotional.*

I won't.

Although I have never experienced serious physical or mental abuse I have known enough people who have. Some people are not crippled by their experienced – scarred, yes, but not crippled. Most of them have survived because they have found hope for the future through their love and friendships with people in the present. They have found one or more people who will trust them, listen to them, encourage them, and support them to move onto a life-time of better experiences.

Other people, however, are crippled for life by the abuse they have experienced and some end up within mental institutions never to expect to experience hope or trust again. Their stories are tragic. Moments of happiness may be all that is available to them unless they are blessed by friendships with people who see beyond the superficial sense of hopelessness to go deeper to the core of the person's ability to crave and offer love and friendship. You and I do not have to limit ourselves to our family and circle of friends to make a difference in someone's life. We can go out and actively search someone who needs our friendship. Our friendship will not erase their memories of being abused, but over time our friendship and the friendship of others may well be a greater source of motivation and hope than the abuse was a cause of de-motivation or of giving up.

Sometimes we cannot help our own family and friends deal with their history of abuse because they will not let us or because we live too far away from each other. In those circumstances, we can use our understanding of what we or others have endured in the way of abuse to search out those who are isolated within their own lives or within actual institutions who can benefit from our presence, our patience and our love.

There is a North American movement called *Citizen Advocacy* that started with the writings of Professor Wolf Wolfensberger of the Training Institute at Syracuse University in New York State. This movement is based on a simple premise: match valued members in society with those who are devalued because of their history, their disabilities, their income level or other form of discrimination. This matching is one of the most effective ways of changing a vulnerable person's life forever. This ongoing, committed contact changes not only the vulnerable person's perception of themselves but also society's perception of the person. The advocate brings all of their knowledge, connections and compassion with them in ways that physically, emotionally and spiritually enhances both their own lives and the person for whom they advocate. I have seen children who were considered 'unfit for adoption' find loving homes. I have seen people wracked with decades of abuse and violence find a home and ultimately satisfying work through such a matching.

I cite only this one example of what is possible to show that no matter the trauma we face, there are ways to deal with it, over time, that can be healing in some ways. As with all the situations we examine in this book, each requires a return to the fundamental beliefs and experiences of happiness, peacefulness, love, joy, wonder, calmness and excitement. I am not talking about the happiness that comes from an ice cream cone in the heat of summer (although that is nice too!). I'm talking about reaching to the core of a person's emotions. The more severe the trauma, the longer it may take. A mother who loses her husband and children in a house fire will not begin rebuilding her life the next day as if nothing significant had happened. A child who was abused by a trusted adult may not overcome their fears within weeks, months or even years. All of life's hardest experiences require similar responses. The craving we see in society 'to belong,' 'to matter' and 'to make a difference' stem from our need to experience positive emotions rather than live the isolating life of self-doubt, guilt, fear and recrimination.

Is there happiness in any of this? Of course there is. There is happiness when a visitor comes to someone who has not seen a loving face for days. There is joy when an abused child finds out there are adults who thrive on their presence and who would fight any battle to secure the child's happiness again. There is happiness when a battered spouse, after years of abuse, finds they can take control over their lives when previous self-doubt promised them only relief through suicide.

In our most difficult times (and we all experience these in one form or another), happiness may be limited to seconds or minutes—but they exist. Their mere existence gives us hope that more happiness is possible. If it was possible before, it may be possible again. We do not even need reassurance that it will happen again — just the hope that it will return is sometimes enough during our darkest hours.

Happiness and Competitiveness

Everyone likes to be a winner! I have never heard anyone shout out with glee *We lost!* When you listen to professional and amateur athletes talk about their biggest game, it is rarely one they lost. When you listen to friends talk about their high school or college memories of the sport, they often talk about when they played their best.

However, if you listen for any length of time, you will also hear these athletes talk about the tough games they lost, the 'bad' calls made by a referee, the 'bad weather,' the 'jet lag' before a game, the 'bad food' that upset their stomachs, etc. etc. They start to make jokes about these 'horror' games and end up laughing, teasing, complaining some more, and moving on to the next game.

We remember the bad with the good. Some of our best lessons are learned during a game that was lost; not won. Many coaches will tell their athletes that they are not taking enough risks during a game; not making enough mistakes to get that big break that leads to a victory.

Steven Nash is one of basketball's greatest players. He had a television ad for a computer company that included some of his playing philosophy. One of which is about excellence and says something like, 'Practice the day after your greatest game.' In other words, he never rests on his laurels but keeps trying to get better. Trying to repeat what he did well in the best game of his life while learning what he can do better in the next game.

The point? Happiness and competitiveness are not just about winning. Although players may initially feel sad, upset, angry, frustrated, disappointed, hurt, betrayed, or more after a big loss, they return to the game in their heads to figure out what to do next time. The best athletes don't concentrate on the negative aspects of losing – they concentrate on what to do better next time around. They are the winners in life's game as well because they take all set backs with that same sense of 'today was bad so let's figure out what to do better tomorrow.'

The best example of this for me was listening to a national athlete talk about playing in a tournament in New Zealand. The athletes, being amateur athletes, didn't have enough money to stay in a hotel so they were billeted with New Zealand players' families. He talked with pride about how tough the games were, how hard everyone played (on both teams) to win and the joys and disappointments at the end of each game. Then he added, *But after the game, we knew we had to go home with these guys and eat with their families so we put the game behind us. We shared food and drink, laughter and teasing, the male bravado of 'We'll get you next time' and had a thoroughly enjoyable time sharing in their lives with their families. That was the essence of that trip. We learned to concentrate and play hard and then, after a few minutes of disappointment if we lost, moved on to a celebration of the other team and their families. It was the best tournament I ever played in.*

This sense of happiness and competitiveness is true in all competitive relationships. Whether it is sports, other types of games, and competitive relationships at work, play and at home. If you spend all of your time competing with colleagues at work, you will have little fun with them. Someone who gets 'promoted above you' can either be your champion at a higher level or your enemy. The happy moments you shared together, the non-competitive aspects of working on a team with each other, together with your inner competitiveness to do a better job personally, are all tools that will help you enjoy and thrive in your work. It is good to be competitive. It is harmful to compete to the point where people don't want to be in the same place with you any more.

I am one of the least competitive people I know – sort of. I don't like to lose any more than the next person but my athletic skills are minimal so I don't often win. It is the same in work situations and at home with my family. I don't want to be competitive with the people I love. I want to support their efforts at excellence not compete against them. I compete with myself. I win when I do something better than I did it before. I lose when I don't/can't give it my all. That competitive drive exists in me but is channelled differently.

That said, if I'm winning at cards, I don't usually let up just to be 'nice.' If I am competing for a contract, I don't give up and let the other company 'win' because I don't like competition. That is not what happiness and competition is about. It is about knowing when to compete and when not to compete. It is about knowing when to enjoy the win without making those who lost feel so bad that you lose relationships over it. The person you beat today in an unkind way, whether in a sport or at work, may be the person you most need when you shift teams or jobs. How many athletes end up playing with a former 'enemy.' Play to win but don't win to harm.

In my working relationships I have a personal motto: anyone I help today may one day help me or help someone else. It is not about getting something back each time you help someone. It is about setting a trend that if I have helped you with something, then maybe you will help someone else down the road. The people who have helped me in my personal and professional lives have not all been 'paid back.' That is impossible. However, their help means I am more able to help others. It is an evolving cycle like the rings of water that move out when a drop hits the pond. When we moved to Canada our next-door neighbor was Dr. Shannon, grandfather of actress Polly Shannon. We didn't speak English or French but he and his family welcomed us and helped us in whatever ways they could. They didn't do it to get some future reward. They did it because it was the right thing to do and it felt good for all of us.

There have been times when I have helped someone only to be hurt by them later on. Some have ignored my request for help. A very few have betrayed my trust. This hurt. It hurt even more when their actions affected my family. Sometimes when I think back to these times, the hurt is almost as fresh as when it happened.

If I took these situations to be what 'the real world was like' then I would ignore all the times I have been helped or have helped others. Those situations were also part of the real world. I cannot deal with everyone as if they are going to hurt me. The odds are that most people are thankful for any help you can offer, just as you are thankful for any help they give in return. The few times it 'backfires' does not make the rule. It is all the times your small and large efforts to help someone in a non-competitive way that shines the light on the joys of working with, rather than against, others.

Happiness and Divorce

In 1980 my mother died. Two years later I spent an afternoon with a dear friend whose parents had recently divorced. We exchanged 'notes' on the experiences we were going through. We both had unanswered questions of why, what could we have done differently and what will happen next.

We both concluded that her experiences were more difficult. My questions had to do with cancer and why my mother got it, what treatments should she have had or not had and how will we deal with her loss. But my situation had an ending to it. My mother died.

My friend's situation was different. There was no ending in sight. Perhaps her parents would reconcile; perhaps not. Perhaps the one parent could overcome the genuine sense of betrayal and years of life spent in a lie. Perhaps both parents would find someone new to love who my friend could accept. There were so many thoughts that began with 'perhaps' and no thoughts that began with certainty.

Neither of us would wish each other's experiences on the other. They were too painful. But in our pain we understood that our experiences were different because I had an ending and a new beginning (however painful) while she had to deal with uncertainty over and over again.

What is the most difficult part of dying for many people? If you ask enough people you will find their greatest difficulty was the uncertainty while awaiting a diagnosis of what was wrong with them. At first my mother thought she was having a mental breakdown because no specialist would acknowledge her symptoms as anything else but anxiety. When she was told of her cancer there was partial relief because finally others recognized what she had feared for months. She did not want to die but she did feel relief at knowing what lay ahead.

This is where people going through a difficult divorce share the experience of those who are dying. They can relate to the uncertainty. They can relate to feeling something inside without finding anyone who will recognize and appreciate what is happening to them.

Can there be any happiness in any of this? By now, you know that my answer is, of course. Again, depending on the depth of hurt and pain involved, it may be only moments of happiness, peacefulness, joy, wonder, calmness or excitement. Sometimes it is expressed as bad jokes like those on the show *M*A*S*H*. Sometimes it is felt through holding a baby in your arms. Even as you wonder what will happen to your baby and the family, there is a comfort in the trusting heart beat next to yours. Sometimes is comes after a terrible nightmare when you wake up and wonder if it was real only to discover that it was not. Sometimes that moment of calmness comes when friends, who have experienced their own difficult divorce, come and tell you that your pain is real and that it won't go away for a while but that they will help you through this.

You know this is true because if you have been divorced, you know that you have brought some happiness and joy to friends going through the same thing. You know that your presence, your experiences, your calmness, and perhaps even your renewed anger at the injustice of it all, helps your friend.

Moments of happiness do not remove pain—they help you through it. Moments of peacefulness or joy do not diminish what you are experiencing—they move you through time so that you can cope. Moments of happiness are not meant to cure all ills or to let you know that you are being silly to suffer so much—they help your recognize your own humanity and remind you that you are not alone—never completely alone.

Some people think that if you have even moments of happiness in times of separation or divorce that you are clearly not suffering as much as you should or that the trauma is really not so bad. It may give some people you know and love an excuse to be less supportive if they see a smile on your face. They may say, *Oh she's doing fine. She doesn't need me.*

However, having more moments of happiness may do the opposite. Having more moments of happiness may draw these same people closer to you as they will be less afraid to be supportive. People fear strong emotions. They fear they will not know what to do. If they see moments of happiness in you, they are more likely to think that they can be helpful. They recognize in you someone who can overcome this difficult time with the right kinds of supports from loving family and friends—and they are right.

Happiness and Evil

There are many people who will tell you that humans are all naturally evil—more naturally evil than good. When you look at the daily news, see how people treat each other in buses or on the roads, listen to how some children treat their parents and vice versa, you can see that it is not hard to argue that people often do bad things before they think to do something good.

Others argue that humans are born good and they learn to do wrong through their environment. They remind you to spend time with a new-born baby to see the genuine and complete joy they experience by being held, by getting their food and by laughing at sights and sounds around them.

The argument about whether or not people are born naturally to take the easy way by cheating, stealing and harming others or not, is unimportant to me. Whichever is true, the consequences of evil are the same. People do bad things. People do good things. What we can look at is how what we believe and what we do encourages people to do a bit more good than they otherwise would.

Barry Neil and Susie Kaufman have argued in several insightful books that *everyone of us is doing the best we can right now with what we know.* We know we are doing things that hurt others or ourselves, but we cannot think of an alternative way to behave that will make us feel as good. So we continue to smoke, drink to excess, take medications and other drugs inappropriately, or we don't exercise. We continue to argue with colleagues at work to get the job done in the way we want it done. We continue to put our work or personal life ahead of our spouse and children even though we know that hurts them. We know better but for us, the alternative is worse. We are doing our best and will not change until either our knowledge, skills or circumstances change.

It is the Kaufmans' belief that people do not make bad decisions but only decisions they think are best right now. They have found that people may change their negative behavior when they look at their own beliefs and find a way to get the same results by being happy. They have worked with children and adults with disabilities, with people who have criminal records for violence, and with people who feel out of control. When some of these people became less judgmental of themselves and of others they were able to feel happier, more productive, more loving and less stressed. The Kaufmans' work (actually loving play) with children who have various disabilities have produced wonderful results for the children, their parents and families.

I recommend their books to you as specific strategies for choosing to be happy more often. They tell stories of children who have been abused or raped, or adults with little or no self-esteem who found ways to be happy in their lives. They tell how some of these people have chosen to change their beliefs and make a difference in how they act. These stories do not guarantee changes for everyone but they are another set of beliefs that do help some people.

Is evil natural? Perhaps. What is more important for me is what we can do to lessen the evil in the world. If people like Dr. Viktor Frankl can find moments of happiness in a concentration camp, then surely most of us can find it in our everyday lives—and more importantly help others to find it too.

Is doing good natural? Perhaps. There are many examples in our lives of people who go beyond typical responses of hate, hurt and harm to help others. Let us learn from them. Let us role model what we learn so that this positive alternative becomes more of a norm than it is now. It is in times of crisis that we often find what is natural in people. During war time, many people did extraordinarily wonderful things to help and protect others. This was especially true at the personal level when people knew each other. When people were strangers and bundled in large groups, it was easier to make them the enemy; the kind of person who was better off dead than alive. We need to re-personalize all human relationships so that no one can be made to be so 'different' that killing them is seen as a good thing.

I have a friend who easily acknowledges that he doesn't like people of a certain culture, as well as those who speak French and those who smoke. He was also very uncomfortable being in the same room with people who have disabilities. This same man will stop on the road or highway whenever someone needs assistance. It doesn't matter their culture, language or whether they are smoking, he stops to help. He has never met an individual person with these characteristics that he doesn't get along with but he still dislikes these various groups of people as a whole.

I once introduced him to another friend of mine who happened to have this culture, speak French as his first language and who smokes. Add to that, this friend's son has what other people label as severe disabilities. I introduced them because my first friend had skills that could help the second friend. Within a short time of working together on home renovations, the men became close friends and have become life-long friends since.

It is getting to know people personally; sharing in their happiness and their dreams for themselves and their families that overcomes prejudice. There is a great song from World War I called *Christmas in the Trenches*. It is based on the true story of how German and English soldiers put down their guns on Christmas Eve in the trenches of Belgium to sing the same Christmas carols (in different languages of course), share chocolate and alcohol, play a game of soccer, and show photos of their loved ones back home. They got to know each other personally. When they returned to war, they rifle aim was very different because, as the song says, *Whose family have I got in my sights?* It is hard to kill a person you know and with whom you have no argument. It is much easier to kill a stranger.

Is evil more natural than good? I do not know. The more important questions are, do you do more good than bad? How can you tip the scales even more in the direction of doing good?

Happiness and Family

Not everyone in the world has a family. Countless people have lost their families through war, hunger, poverty, hatred, and illness. Many people talk about a family of friends as a replacement for their own families.

People who do not have their own families near them have lost a major part of their history; their belonging to a historical unit. No one can replace that. RECOGNIZING THAT LOSS IS NOT THE SAME THING AS ALWAYS BEING UNHAPPY THAT YOU NO LONGER HAVE A FAMILY.

My parents died in the early 1980s. I miss them terribly. I think of them every day even though few people ever mention their names in my company any more. I miss not hearing about them. I miss not being part of their family anymore. I used to be very unhappy about them not being here…so unhappy that I missed opportunities to share happiness with people who were still alive and with me now. I do not make that mistake anymore. Cherish the love around you. You don't forget those who have died but neither must you forget those still here with you now.

I have very little family in Canada and have been very fortunate to have my mother's cousin living only two hours away. Although our families were close growing up, we have become even closer. I call her *Aunt* and her husband *Uncle* and our children call them *Oma* and *Opa*. Their children, my 2nd cousins, and their own families have been extraordinarily warm in including my family in such major events as Christmas, Easter and Thanksgiving dinners and the major birthdays and anniversaries. They have all opened their hearts and their family to us and we are genuinely grateful for their thoughtfulness and kindness and their wonderful sense of humor. We share hundreds of memories of laughter, joy, great food and of being together through good times and bad. Their own hardships confirm my belief that cherishing the ones still with you does nothing to diminish your love of those loved ones who have died.

Another person has helped fill a family void through her thoughtfulness and sense of common history. I helped my aunt in Holland take care of her father (my grandfather) when he was ill and helped him live at home until he died. She has opened up her heart and home to my wife and later our son and daughter. We have stayed with her for one-to-three month visits and she helped teach our children to ride a bike, explore Holland's beautiful nature and surroundings. The mere mention of her pancakes is enough to bring a smile to my children's faces. She has pretended to enjoy watching soccer games with our son and encouraged my daughter's creativity by opening up a 'secret' room in the attic where she could use her wildest imagination uninterrupted. Her home is a safe haven in a busy and often complex world. We learn a great deal from her and she from us. This mutual gift binds us eternally. Happiness is our bond as well as the help we offer each other in times of need. She is a kindred spirit and a joy to be with even though she lives much too far away!

A family of friends is not a replacement for a family. They are a different kind of family and one that is also irreplaceable as well. Different people will enter and leave that family of friends but each one leaves memories behind and each one reminds us that being loved, appreciated, recognized and needed are important elements to being happy.

My best friend since Grade Nine has taught me a great deal about what a family of friends is all about. We are as different as two friends can be. We differ in our work, our politics, our religion, our cultural history, and our physical abilities. What we share is a friendship of love and acceptance. We both would like to take on some of the qualities of the other. We also have a friendship of being there for the other. When my mother was rushed to the hospital for the last time while I was in Quebec City, he was there with my father until I could arrive. My sister's best friend in Canada was also there (a similar, wonderful friendship) without us. They were my father's strength when he was alone. My friend hates hospitals more than I do but he put his fears and anxieties aside to be there for my father and later, for me. He was a shoulder to cry on, literally–a friend to lean on.

Another type of memory happened when I turned 35. Janet, my wife, surprised me with a birthday party. She arranged to have people go to a downtown Toronto bar where I was billed as the entertainment for the night. When I got there (supposedly to help celebrate another friend's birthday) I was speechless. As the evening went on and I saw so many happy faces and people sharing in my birthday a friend came up to me and said, *Your parents would have loved to have been here for this. They would have been so happy for you.*

She was right of course. They would have

been so happy and proud. In one sense they were there in the faces of our relatives and friends. They were there in a spiritual sense that was powerful and comforting. More than a few times that night I wished that they could have been there physically to share in my excitement and joy. I was not unhappy that they were not there however. You just had to look around the room to see how lucky I was and how blessed I felt. The memories of that evening will help me through difficult times for years to come. The memory of those people's smiles and laughter showed me the power and influence of a family of friends. Certainly such a family will change with time but not in importance. Thank you to all who shared in that night!

Happiness and Fear

Many authors have written that the opposite of love is not hate but fear. People do the worst things imaginable out of fear. Some of these fears include a fear of: poverty, rejection, dying, loosing loved ones, God, power and authority, and the fear of not being valued. When we trace some of the horrors of history it may be helpful to examine what some people call evil and see if the true root of that evil is actually fear.

For those of you who know me you know that I have written about and for people who are dying. We can learn so much from people who have a limited time left with us. Rose Levit, in her book about her daughter, *Ellen: A Short Life Long Remembered* quotes from a letter Ellen wrote to a friend:

When there is fear, there is no love. Along with fear comes distrust, suspicion, hate. With the absence of fear you have freedom— love.What is life —it is such a complex thing and yet at the same time so simple—it's silly to pin a definition on it. If you can under- stand all these complex things—fear, freedom, love—and still at the same time keep your mind simple—and love the beauty of a sunny day, just because it is a sunny day—then you can truly be free.

Fears are the greatest block to being happy. Overcoming fears requires courage and per- sistence. It requires a belief system that under- stands the power we give our own fears. It requires time, perspective and a strong philos- ophy to fight when we are weakest. It helps to spend some of our time when we are strongest to understand why we need the fear. When we find out why we need fear we may be able to replace it with an equally powerful feeling of self-love and happiness.

I have a tremendous fear of hospitals and sickness. I have seen perhaps too much of both to believe that I would have control over my health and happiness while I was sick. It is a fear I am overcoming with time, effort, perspective and support just as I got over my almost crippling fear that my parents would die young. They did die young but I continue to thrive through the memory of their love and support and the love of my wife and children.

I am reminded that pain and suffering sometimes leads to happiness or that pain and suffering do not rule out happiness. These emotions are not always at opposite ends of our emotions. Falling in love, getting married, raising children, accomplishing professional challenges, remaining devoted to our beliefs, giving of ourselves in civic and charitable work all may involve some suffering. Children get sick, our spouses are not always perfect (either are we!), our work does not always go well, and so on. Would we give up some of that suffering if we knew we would never fall in love, if we would never see the trust and love in a child's eye, if we would never see the love shared during a time of grief? I do not think so.

Happiness does not exclude other feelings. HAPPINESS CAN GIVE SOME SENSE OF PERSPECTIVE AND HELP US USE ALL OF OUR EMOTIONS TO THEIR FULL BENEFIT. Fear prevents any of our emotions from helping ourselves or others. We have all overcome certain fears. We can overcome others.

Happiness and God

I do not belong to a specific church or religion. My spiritual beliefs are rooted in Judeo-Christian philosophies as well as the wisdom found in ancient texts. I have seen the wonderful comfort, support and direction that organized religion has given so many people. I have great respect for spiritual leaders and followers who use their belief to do good.

Faith is invaluable. Mother Theresa has said that her primary spiritual role was to help Catholics be better Catholics, Hindus better Hindus and Buddhists better Buddhists. The spirit of those sentiments is what I try to follow.

There is a little book by a young man named Fynn. He called it *Mister God This is Anna*. It is a wonderful book about a real little girl's faith in God and her constant search for wonder in the slums of London in the 1930s. It summarizes better than anything I have read what I believe in. When studying French in Quebec City in 1980, the teacher passed around a blank page and asked us each to write down our favorite book. The woman who became my wife wrote down: *Mister God This is Anna!*

Let me give you a few examples of this young girl's wisdom:

The difference from a person and an angel is easy. Most of an angel is in the inside and most of a person is on the outside. (p. 13)

And God said love me, love them, and love it, and don't forget to love yourself. (p 33) This sentence is what world religions talk about. Loving yourself is one of the hardest things to do. Believing in God as a friend might help you see yourself as God does.

Anna was not only deeply in love with Mister God; she was proud of him. Anna's pride in Mister God grew and grew to such dimensions that in some idiot moment I wonder if Mister God ever went pink with pleasure. Whatever feelings people have about Mister God over the many centuries, I'm very sure of one thing, nobody has ever liked Mister God more than Anna. (p. 50) Many people talk about God, many people believe in God. Fewer people believe God and see God as a friend they can like and love.

A childlike, not childish, belief in God, or whatever you might call a divine creator is a simple belief—not necessarily an easy one to practice. It requires us to examine our beliefs and expectations of our faith and concentrate on the most basic and important aspects of our faith. It requires us to remember childlike wonder and faith. It challenges us to break through the many *shoulds* and *should nots* to find out what is really important.

Anna believed that people spent too much time talking about the Bible and too little time acting upon the lessons within the Bible. She felt that people missed out on a profound and wonderful friendship with Mister God. She believed that God is the only friend we have who knows us from the inside out and who loves us no matter what we do. Anna's childlike belief in God is different than what many of us learned. If we read many of the things that the great spiritual teachers have said we would find that they, and Anna, have similar beliefs about the power of a child's faith in God.

I have heard of a scholar who translated the Dead Sea Scrolls from the original Aramaic (the language Jesus spoke). His translations were different than the ones we are used to reading. What interested me most was how he translated the 10 Commandments. When I first learned the commandments in elementary school I thought it strange that we would need special rules to tell us not to steal, lie or kill. These were obvious. The thought of actually killing someone had not even entered my mind until then.

This translator, (I wish I knew his name) said that the commandments were not meant as rules at all. He said the original text began with, *If you love me, then...* In other words, the text said that if you loved God you would not think to lie, steal or kill. Rather than the 10 Commandments, the 10 phrases became *consequences* of a deep and profound love of God. That makes sense to me and, I suspect, would make sense to many young children. If you do not believe in God, the thought of these rules becoming consequences still holds. If you love this planet, the human family we belong to, your own family and friends, and yourself, then you will not steal from others, kill people or the environment, nor lie to harm others.

You would be filled with love and goodness and act accordingly. Just as in classical philosophy, when you know what the good life is you will know how to act. *When you are filled with love of God or nature, of others and of yourself you will know right from wrong.* This is a simple idea that takes a lot of practice and faith. I am working on it.

Happiness and Grief

Of all the concepts about happiness that I found most difficult was the idea that you could grieve someone's death and still be happy. It seemed too strange an idea. It was certainly not one I was interested in learning when I was going through the grief of both my parents deaths and my grandfather's death, all within five years. My thoughts changed as I spent some time thinking about how happiness and grief could work together. I will need to give you a little bit of personal history first from a series of Christmases.

In 1979 I was a student in Quebec City. My sister was returning to Toronto from Germany with her new husband and we were going to have our first family Christmas as an extended family. I was poor as many students are and did not know what I could get my parents to tell them how proud I was of them and how much I loved them and how glad I was that our family would be all together again.

Poverty brings out the poetry in people so I wrote my parents a song; one of the first songs I ever wrote. Several of the lines are:

We always know we are never alone.
If we suffer or if we are lonely,
It is because we haven't given our love
wholly.
We always know we are never alone, because
you are here.

It seems ironic now that I chose those words because, as history unfolded, that was my last present to my mother. She died the following April.

The first Christmas after my mother died I was in Holland helping my grandfather who was ill. It was a special time with a special man. I missed being with my father for our first Christmas without my mother but we had both agreed that I was needed more in Holland. My grandfather died the following July.

The next few Christmases were special with my father. We missed some of the beauty of those days, however, because of the sadness we felt at missing my mother. My mother was my kindred spirit. We did not have to talk a lot with each other because we often knew how the other felt. I was a mommy's boy in the most loving interpretation of that phrase. I missed her (and continue to miss her) like few others. So did my father.

In 1983 my future wife and I had a family Christmas with my father. It was a wonderful and special time that I am so grateful for. It was only four years since our last complete family Christmas but it was a time for my Dad, my fiancée and I that I will treasure always. My father and I lived together and we had become very close during the time after my mother was ill. We both loved her very much. We both lost our best friend and her loss brought us closer together. He became a best friend, mentor and advisor whose constant encouragement helped me through the failure of my first business. He was the kind of father that I hoped to be to my children. We did not know it that Christmas, but it was our last Christmas together.

The point in telling you all of this is an obvious one. You will have heard this point many times in your life—live each day as if it were your last one with the people you love. IN MISSING MY MOTHER, THEN MY GRANDFATHER AND NOW MY FATHER I SOMETIMES FIND THAT I MISS THE BEAUTY AND SPECIAL LOVE OF THOSE PEOPLE I DO SHARE CHRISTMAS WITH NOW. In thinking too much about wonderful memories of the past, I have sometimes missed the opportunity to create new memories and to value the family of relatives and friends who are still with me.

We need time to grieve someone's death and their absence from special holidays and events. We need to take the time to feel our loss and to recognize that we do this grieving to help ourselves, not to help the person who has died. At the same time that we grieve we can also take a loving look around the rest of our family, friends, and people we work with. We can imagine ourselves 5, 10 or 50 years later. How do we want to remember these special holidays and events? How do we want to remember the people with whom we did celebrate? Perhaps they will not be there in 5 or 10 years. In our grief do we stop ourselves from sharing some happiness with those who we may grieve years later? If my grandfather had grieved his wife's death intensely for the years remaining of his life, I would never have met him or discovered a kindred spirit.

Looking into the future may not be possible when experiencing intense grief. There will come a time, however, when looking into the future is possible again.

What I am suggesting is not easy to do. The idea of concentrating on the present when our grief is so raw is not easy. It will take effort. All of us have so much to be grateful for that we should not waste our limited time on earth living and remembering only the past. Enjoy creating the memories of these special times and everyday so that you can use those memories at another time when you will need them.

We always know that we are never alone. My parents may not be physically with me at Christmas or any other time of year but my parents are always with me and I am truly never alone. They gave me a wonderful gift over many years of living together and I did not fully recognize until that last Christmas together in 1979. That last Christmas with my father in 1983 reminded me of the gift they gave me of happy memories of childhood, the memories of their love and pride, and the memories of their happiness with me. They continually teach me to be a better husband, father, friend, neighbor and human being.

Happiness and Job Loss

When my father found out he had life-threatening emphysema, he was fired from his job as a property manager. It was not quite that brutal. The right words of concern were expressed: *You shouldn't tax your energy at work anymore. Go home and be with your family.* He received a 'package' but lost his reason for getting up in the morning. Nothing devastated him as much as losing his job and regular contact with the people with whom he worked. His worth was defined, in his mind, but the productive work he could still do. He was denied the ability to show usefulness at a time when self-worth was most at question. His death was hastened, I believe, by his losing his job.

Is that putting job loss too strongly? If you

ask people who lose their jobs what it feels like they will use many of the same words that people use who are going through grief. They will describe physical symptoms of chest pain, breathing difficulty, muscle strain, nausea, sleeplessness and more. People trying to be helpful will say things like, *You can always get another job* or *Don't let them get to you — show them they were wrong.* These are good sentiments but not helpful ones when you are going through the loss of your personal identity.

The reactions of people who lose their jobs will not be the same of course. Losing a job you didn't like but knowing that someone else is ready to hire you is one thing. It is not the same as someone who has worked for 12 years for the same company doing their best work but still is downsized. Job loss can be physically and emotionally painful. Even if you quit a job on principle, the resulting feelings of loss are real.

So why do so many people a year or two after job loss say, *That was the best thing that ever happened to me.* Why do other people say *That was the worst thing that ever happened to me.*

Age and life experience may have a lot to do with this. The likelihood that you can find work again or start your own business may help people while others are paralyzed by a society that sees older workers as a handicap. Sometimes it is just luck or friends that help people find something better to do than they were doing. Sometimes it is the trauma of the loss that forces people to remember what their career goals used to be and return to some that now appear more likely to succeed.

It is not just about perspective. Sometimes losing your job forces you to recognize that you were in the wrong place and at the wrong time. Sometimes losing your job reinforces that your job skills are not as transferable as you had hoped and that you may need retraining. Sometimes, you reach a certain age and know that very few jobs exist for someone of your experience and salary expectations.

Is there happiness in any of this? Of course,

but again the situation and your personality will determine how long your moments of happiness, peacefulness, joy, bliss, calmness and excitement will be. Your financial needs will determine how much fear and anxiety job loss creates. You may go through the loss of your home (if you can't keep up the payments) or other possessions. You may need to move to a different town or city. You may need to change your career altogether and live with less. Or you may discover that you have what it takes to work on your own and, perhaps, earn more than you ever did before.

I cannot tell you which circumstance will be true for you. I do know there are people who can help with career planning, financial planning, job searches and more. I know that an attitude of hopefulness and happiness is more likely to help you succeed at a job inter-view than one of hopelessness and unhappi-ness. I know that my parents did not have the jobs they wanted but as uneducated immigrants without much English they were limited in their choices but not limited in how they did their work.

Anytime you come into contact with people (and what job does not) you have an opportunity for happiness. My parents taught me that no job is menial if you can bring some joy to people's lives. You don't hang your head when you wash an apartment lobby floor—you raise it, you look people in the eye because you are doing an honest day's work and you try to bring a smile to their face. When you succeed, your job has achieved a higher level of importance in the day-to-day lives of others and of yourself.

As apartment building Superintendents, my parents came into contact with many people. They touched people's lives and were touched in return. One young boy would not go to school unless my father (who was usually in the lobby at school time) helped put on his coat. Some people would not make life decisions without first listening to my parents' inherent wisdom. Their job title did not represent the importance of their lives to other people.

Happiness, then, at a time of job loss is found in finding ways to connect with other people. Your typical response at losing your job may to isolate yourself and overindulge in food, drink or drugs. That initial response may be necessary given how you have dealt with other losses in your life, but to survive, this period of isolation must be a short one. You must connect with people who can bring a momentary smile to your face. Connect with people who value your company. Connect with people who have overcome a similar fate. Search out others who are going through the same thing now and share the experience of rising above the loss together.

One of the reasons some people say that job loss was the best thing that ever happened to them is because the loss forced them to be more alert to their day-to-day life, to the people within that life and the circumstances surrounding them. They had to deal with spouses and children and their fears. They had to re-examine their dreams to see if any could now come true. They found out that living for today doesn't mean ignoring the past or the future but to be truly alive to all the day's experiences – to look a child in the face and to ask if you can share part of that day with them that you normally would not have had time for when you were working.

Job loss or job change is one of the best times to sit down with a financial planner and examine how you really want to live your life from this day forward. In my case, when I resigned a well paying job on principle, I discovered that family was more important than working full time so I began to save more for retirement and have that nest egg in the background whenever I turned down a full-time position. I have worked part-time for over 25 years now (with many financial ups and downs) but I never look back with regret because I have memories of time spent with my wife, children, other family and friends. These are invaluable memories that money can never replace. We do with less. We own less. We go out less and yet our lives feel so much richer and enjoyable. It may not be for you, but the process is the same. Find out how you want to live and use job loss or career change as an opportunity to fulfil your dreams.

Happiness and Organizations

I once taught a course in laughter and play in a large institution. I was told afterward the Board of Directors had heard about the successful workshop and were not the least bit happy. They said there was no room for this happiness and laughter stuff in their organization. After all they did 'serious' business there and could not let laughter get in the way of productivity and service.

I treat my business, teaching and writing very seriously. I try not to make it too solemn though. I believe people need to express their happiness, excitement, or joy at work. I also believe they need to express their disappointment, anger or unhappiness. I certainly try not to take myself too seriously. We are on this planet a very short time and if we live in this 'real world' too solemnly we will end our lives regretting may missed opportunities.

An organization is not a living thing. When we swear loyalty to our workplace or country, we should not be swearing allegiance to a thing. People make up organizations. All organizations recognize that fact in their senior management's policies and public relations. Many organizations that talk loudest about how much they value their staff behave in inconsistent ways which speaks much more loudly than their words.

Just as people need a set of beliefs and morals to guide their decisions, so do organizations. Many organizations now use mission statements, strategic and operational plans to outline their beliefs and actions. I am willing to bet that if I interviewed 1,000 managers and staff in a random selection of organizations, that most of them would not be able to quote their mission statement and most would certainly not sit in meetings and use their missions statement as a guideline to help them make day-to-day decisions. Many mission statements may have 'respect for customers and staff' as one of their philosophic principles but when it comes to making decisions how many quote this respect for customers and staff before making important decisions?

It is not that organizations, or rather the people that manage them, purposefully do bad things to customers and staff. They have grown into organizations that value policies and procedures created in one era without regard to current circumstances. They need help to remember what their mission is and to act accordingly.

ALMOST WORSE THAN 'BAD ORGANIZA-TIONS,' I THINK, ARE ONES THAT ARE CONTENT TO BE AVERAGE ONES. Average organizations argue that they are no worse at treating people than other organizations. Sadly, they may be right. There is much talk about a search for excellence or benchmarking excellence but it usually translates into a search for financial success often at the cost of devaluing people. Average organizations allow negligence, poor working relationships and apathy to exist. Out of these conditions comes many of the evil things that occur in the world. Nazi politicians and military people did not start the euthanasia projects in Germany. They were started by scientists and psychiatrists who took average health care organizations, and over time, convinced enough average people, to accept the massive genocide of their fellow Germans. These Germans were initially people with disabilities and disfiguring characteristics, then when most of those had been killed, people with mental illnesses were added to the list and those with opposing political views. It was only after so many of these people died that the Nazis turned to the annihilation of German Jews and Jews in conquered countries.

In modern times, average organizations are harder to turn around if the leadership has weak foresight and a weak understanding of how they have control over the working environment. Individuals do have control over how they react to situations, their work environment and their boss but people can also be worn down – *their* MORALE *weakens when their* MORALS *are constantly tested*. Average organizations, and therefore, average managers and staff must recognize their power – personally and professionally. If more managers who live in 'the real world' of bottom lines and financial accountability concentrated some of their efforts on being happier a bit more often themselves, they would see a domino effect throughout the whole organization.

Happiness is 'real world.' People who are happy in their work *are more productive, are more responsive* to the needs of clients and customers, *are more supportive* of management, and *are more consistent* in how they make decisions. Funny thing too, happy people tend to be better at financial accountability.

Happiness and Poverty / Starvation

Many of us have travelled or seen documentaries of places where there is great poverty and starvation. Do we have the right to be happy while others suffer? Is our happiness something that we take from other people so they have none themselves? Is there a limited amount of happiness in the world and am I having more than my fair share? Or is happiness something inside of us that we can choose to use for personal satisfaction and/or for helping others? Is our happiness better than the happiness that we might find in a very poor section of Calcutta?

Poverty, starvation, death by the millions each year are not things we can change by feeling guilty or unhappy. These are horrible events that we can change. We can actually end world poverty. Whether we are happy or not is not the real question. The question is what is it we need to feel in order to make a difference? People with a religious calling are not the only people able to make a difference. People who feel guilty or anger at injustice are not the only ones who can improve the world.

What is a wrong response, however, is to use so much of our energy to feel angry and sad at the overwhelming injustices in the world to the point where we have no energy left to make changes. We may be great water cooler problem solvers but it still takes real action, or supporting others who are making the changes necessary, to change the world.

Happiness can be a wonderful motivator to help us change our world. We can be happy as we help people near to us or help those we may never see. There are many ways we can help: financially, through volunteer work, through spiritual work, through our career choices, through our political and spiritual connections, through prayer, and, of course, through friendship and love. All of these are possible while you are happy or unhappy. The choice truly is yours. It is not even an either or situation. You can just choose to be happier more often than you are now when dealing with world issues.

Happiness and the Real World

Aaah, the 'real world.' These two words may be the greatest blocks to our being happier. People use these two words as freely as they use love. They cannot define the real world except to say that it is complex, difficult, hard and filled with insolvable problems. Some of these people see that happiness is possible in the real world but only for short periods of time. After all there is work to do, injustices to right, money to save and old age to worry about.

I think that some people who live in the real world have confused fun with happiness. As I said before, fun is something you feel during an activity and fun activities are things you may not be able to do all day, every day. Just think for a minute about some of the glamorous movie stars you have read about. They go to huge parties, drink and eat the best there is, and live in glorious mansions where servants do all the hard work. Wherever they go people recognize them, praise them and ask them for autographs. Their home towns want to have parades in their honor, they receive awards, and they can afford surgery to improve their noses, stomachs and thighs so they do not have to worry about getting old like you and I do.

Some people would argue that these glamorous stars do not live in the real world either. They are having fun all the time while the rest of us have to work for a living. Let us look at these stars a bit more carefully.

When they are working on a play or film they often have to get up at five or six in the morning and work late into the evening. They have to be glamorous when what they may really want is a normal life where they can go and do what they please without having to have security guards and newspeople following them around. They have an extremely high rate of divorce, drug and alcohol abuse, troubled children and, as many autobiographies reveal, a deep sense of loneliness.

These may be the people who are having fun in all those magazine pictures but they are often a far way from being happy.

The real world can be lonely, frightening and boring. It does not have to be. Anyone who has survived incest, abuse, war, poverty, or other difficult events in their lives know that those events are only part of the real world. These same people have also experienced love, warmth, friendship, laughter and joy. Those are also feelings that we have in the real world.

My father had an understanding of the real world. He was a teenage farm boy during World War II. On the morning of the Nazi invasion he looked up from milking a cow to see a young soldier standing behind him with a rifle pointed at him. *Attention!* the soldier yelled. My dad nearly wet his pants. He was 15 years old. Later in the war he was caught smuggling, with his older brother, goods across the border (they lived only a few miles from the German border). I am not sure if my father's gift of gab came to him that day or before, but they talked their way out of a firing squad!

After the war Holland was still a colonial power and Indonesia was one of their colonies. My father was drafted to fight there for two years when he was 22-24 years old. He had lost much of his youth to war.

After he returned from Indonesia he married my mother and three children later (my oldest sister died of measles before I was born) our family immigrated to Canada without speaking a word of English between us. My father broke his arm within 10 weeks of our arrival so, without workers' compensation and unemployment insurance at the time, we lost most of our savings. They were hard years for my parents yet they kept it from us. My sister and I were on an adventure!

Without stretching this story out too long, the next few decades were filled with hard work and trying to raise two children in a new country. My parents became apartment building superintendents so that they could be close to home and still work together. When my mother became too ill to work anymore my dad was promoted to a property manager. Seven years later his wife died in their bedroom at home and our lives changed dramatically.

When my father became ill he felt badly about two things. The first was that he felt it was unfair for his son to have to experience the death of both parents and his grandfather all within five years. That really hurt him. The second thing that upset my father was not that he was dying or that he had lost his job but that he could not come to my wedding in 7 months. We talked a lot about that. We did not pretend that he would be able to go and we did not pretend that he was getting well when he was not. Because we did not pretend we were able to get his help in planning part of the wedding. He was able to give my wife a wedding present—a treasured necklace my mother used to wear.

He was able to talk to me about his hopes and dreams for my future. He was able to hug me and kiss me and tell me he would miss me but that I would be okay. He never doubted my abilities and continued to encourage my dreams to write and teach.

This chapter is about the real world. My dad knew a lot about the real world. He was not an idealist and saw much of the horror and injustices in the world. He recognized that he could only affect small parts of that world. He knew that I would miss him and my mother terribly when it came time for the wedding. He knew he could not be there to help me through the happiest, and potentially, saddest days of my life. My fiancé had never met my mother and now she would not see my father at our wedding.

My sister and my father were kindred spirits of a sort. They understood how the other thought and they were both great sentimentalists (it runs in the family!). I suspect that my sister suggested it to my father or at least helped him to find a way to help me at my wedding. She wrote a wedding card for us on his behalf. Whether they were his words directly or she wrote what she thought he wanted to say, the card is invaluable. I received it the night before my wedding. For a short time my parents were with me in that motel room in Qualicum Beach. The words were perfect. Exactly what I needed to hear. They were his famous hugs but in words. I cried like a baby and was comforted by those tears. The next day I walked on a Vancouver Island east-coast beach and thought of my parents, our family and our history. That card helped me immensely. Later at my wedding I had the time of my life. I married the right person. My sister, her family, my special aunt (who gave me away that day) and some wonderful cousins from Holland were there. I could not have been happier. My parents were there too, thanks to that card. The real world did not have to be sad that day. The real world was a happy world that day. My wife, our families and special friends there and throughout the world, and my dad made sure it was.

If we examine anyone's life and try to give a percentage to how often they were happy and how often they were unhappy what do you think the average percentages would be? Do you want to be an average person in our real world? What percentage of the time are you happy? Do you want to increase that percentage? What is stopping you? Some interesting questions, eh? Like my father, perhaps you can think of ways to help other people be happier more often and in doing that you will be happier too.

Happiness and Self-Image

When you look in the mirror, are you happy with how you look?

I was in a course once where the teacher asked everyone who was happy with how they looked to raise their hand. After a very long minute or so of giggles and silence, one brave soul raised his hand and said, *I was happy with how I looked 10 years ago when I worked in construction!* Everyone laughed along with him to relieve the real tension on the room. None of us were pleased with how we looked.

Why is that? The quick answer is that none of us fit the body ideal that corporations have determined we need to follow—young, too thin, the perfect nose and gleaming white teeth, sexy, wide-eyed, with gorgeous hair and skin. Why this model of what defines beauty? Well if our role model of beauty was more of what we actually looked like, where would those companies be that promote beauty products, plastic surgery, weight loss programs, and some fountain of youth alternative health products?

We define an unattainable model of beauty so that we have to spend billions of dollars per year trying to look somewhat closer to that ideal. In fact, globally, we spend about $38 billion on hair care products, $24 billion on skin care, $18 billion on makeup, and $15 billion on perfumes. That is $95 billion dollars on just products.[1] Add to that courses, weight loss programs, surgery and the like and we spend more on how we look than many countries spend annually on all of their social, health and education programs combined!

It is stupid. We know that it is stupid. We try to teach our children it is stupid. And

[1] Audrey Brashich. (2006). *All Made Up.* New York: Walker and Company, p. 64.

yet...what they see are adults trying to look younger, act younger, and avoid becoming the wise people in the community by acting like teenagers with a budget! What else explains the money we waste acquiring clothes, makeup, shoes and stuff to look and feel good? What if women had a few more pounds and curves and loved it? What if men thought that balding was a sign of becoming wiser rather than impotent? What if the size of penises and breasts did not define sexual attractiveness? What if we trusted nature a little more and beauty corporations a little less? What if we spent the money we wasted on beauty products and used it to travel the world (a better use of our economic power) and make a difference in the lives of others (an even better use of our economic power!) What if we treated our elders with respect rather than condescension? What if our children learned to treat us with more respect rather than condescension?

What if...?

Realistically though, are we likely to individually go against all the public demands of who is beautiful and who is not? Probably not! I'll still try to lose some weight and build muscles. I'll still buy clothes I think my wife will like me in. But I will also do more!

I will try to become happier, more often, with how I look and I will remember, more often, that some of the sexiest people we know do not fit the modern culture's view of beauty. Why is that? I know that I have often been attracted to women who do not fit the norm but who are stunning nonetheless. You probably can look at the Hollywood models and see beauty but also be aroused and attracted by men or women at the local store, school, neighborhood as well. Why?

Why is someone like a Bill Cosby or Bill Clinton attractive to so many women even though they don't always fit the ideal of a young, athletic, perfect-skin-and-hair kind of guy? Why does Queen Latifa or Gloria Steinman turn men's heads? Why are the people you like to ogle in magazines not the kind of person you want to take home to meet yor mother?

It is because, corny as it sounds, we know that someone's personality, their sense of power, their own positive self-image, their humor, knowledge and graces are all attractions to us. If someone sees themselves as attractive more often, more people are attracted to them–regardless of how much they weigh, how tall they are, what age they are, whether they are bald or have cellulite. Some of the sexiest women I know may be defined as overweight or pear shaped yet how they dress and carry themselves are immensely attractive to men because these women dress, behave and reflect an outer and inner beauty as they define it. I know men who are balding, older, and not particularly fit who attract others to them because they are funny, good listeners, and thoughtful. Their bodies pour out inner and outer qualities that we admire and aspire to.

Ultimately, those people who reflect an inner quality of self-acceptance and inner peace radiate a sense of themselves that attracts almost everyone around them. Mother Teresa, the Dalai Lama and other spiritual leaders certainly do not dress or carry themselves as corporate ideal body models, but they do attract people to them.

The reverse is also true that beauty, as defined by corporations, does not lead to more happiness for everyone. There are many biographies written of the beautiful people to show that although they enjoyed some of their celebrity, and certainly their wealth, they missed out on happy marriages, children who loved them, people who trusted them and whom they could trust. That does not mean that all beautiful people, as defined by our culture, are unhappy. Many find happiness not because of their beauty but in spite of it. They find spouses and friends who see them for who they are rather than what our culture tells them they should be.

So when you look in the mirror, what should you do to feel happier about how you look? Here is my top ten list, for what it is worth:

1. Stop looking in the mirror so often. Who you see is not who other people see anyway. You rarely see your profile yet most of the people you meet see a great deal of it. What you see in the mirror is a reflection, therefore, the opposite of what most people see. Check you hair, make sure there are no broccoli florets hanging from your mouth and move on. At most, you need to check yourself in the mirror only a few times a day. Obsess about something more important to your happiness.

2. Accentuate what you find attractive about yourself without spending a lot of money doing it. I know a woman who can go to a used clothing store, pick out a lovely blouse, change the buttons with some other ones she has a home and have a beautiful new blouse. She is a senior executive in a large corporation who hates wasting money!

3. Tell the people you love you need some positive reinforcements about how you look. Tell them you need more hugs and compliments (genuine ones–not superficial ones) to show you they think you are attractive. The difference on the face of a friend who perceived herself as unattractive once she met her future husband who thinks she is stunning has been wonderful to see. We see ourselves often through the eyes of those we love and who love us. Help them see you better and return the favor.

4. Spend time with older people. Not only can you learn from them, they will always see you as younger and fun to be with! They value your company rather than judge how you look (at least most of them will!)

5. Recognize that signs of aging in your body are not a reflection of who you are. It is a natural process. Glorify in it. Stay healthy and become fitter so you can enjoy your body even more. Enjoy your physical sensations–all of them.

6. Look at your young children and you will see the beauty in them. Recognize that your elders (parents, aunts and uncles, grandparents) see you in the same light. Your young children also see Mom or Dad and not your physical strengths and weaknesses. They don't look at your external or internal beauty alone—they combine them and see the person that is you just as you do with your children. Look at yourself through their eyes.

7. Spend time with a pet—who else sees you in all your glory with unconditional love (as long as you love and feed them!).

8. Make a genuine effort to read less glamor magazines, gossip magazines (I used to be addicted to *The National Enquirer*), television and movies. This is where corporations spend the most money to convince you that you need their help to look beautiful. It isn't true!

9. Spend more time with people who like who they are rather than with people who are

never satisfied with who they are or what they look like.

10. Lastly, and most importantly, learn to be happier more often. There are few things as attractive in a person as their happiness and general sense of feeling good about being who they are. They attract us because we want to be more like them—not their looks, but their character and their sense of who they are; their self-image.

Happiness and Self-Talk

We constantly sabotage our lives, our work, our relationships, and our self-image by what we say to ourselves. Whether we do it quietly in our minds or out loud in anger, it has the same effect. For example, how many times have you said to yourself: *You dummy. How could you be so stupid!* This could be after forgetting your house keys or misplacing your wallet or forgetting an important birthday or anniversary? I recently forgot the name of a person I have known for over 15 years. My mind was elsewhere and trying to remember that name was a huge frustration.

Some of our self-talk is more harmful. A friend in high school was told by a teacher that: *You are just not smart enough for university dear. Better go to college and pick something easy like working with children.You'd be good at that.*

My friend listened rather than rebelled. Her own self-talk had already told her that she was not very smart even though she was a leader at school and in her volunteer work. This teacher confirmed my friend's self-talk, rather than created it. She did go to college and found out she liked learning more than she thought. She was also good at it! She worked in Early Childhood Education for a few years but decided she wanted to learn more. So she went to university and got her Bachelor's Degree in Psychology. Not satisfied yet, she went on to her Masters and finally her Ph.D. She is now an internationally known speaker and therapist in children's grief.

You can bet that her self-talk did not improve overnight. It took years of effort to overcome negativity but she did it. Knowing her through those years I also know that she was happy for much of it as she followed her dream, overcame difficulties in several areas and became able to help many young people deal with their grief. She laughed often, comforted more often and shared her experiences and learning with colleagues from around the world.

So what do you say to yourself? What doubts or negative judgements prevent you from being happy more often?

I still catch myself using self-talk that is defeatist and harmful. We all do it. I knew a senior executive of a large manufacturing firm who was retiring. He was the chief operating officer and had a large, lovely office in downtown Toronto. I asked him what had worried him during his career. His answer: *I always worried that someone would find out I did not know as much as they thought I knew.* Even in his position, with his power and influence and his excellent service to that company for decades, his self-talk had told him he was never good enough.

A woman I have known for over 25 years has constantly told herself and others around her that she is in pain, is unhappy, is worried and that her life has had little value—for over 25 years. She raised her children, did part-time work and volunteer work, has been a dear friend to many and helped many others, but mostly without a smile. She has missed out so much and no amount of support or encouragement has convinced her otherwise. It has been sad to watch.

Compare that to another woman I have known for over 50 years who was orphaned at a young age, institutionalized in a mental hospital because the system could not find her a home, who was kept in the institution for longer than normal because she was a good cleaner (free labor), who married late and had 5 children, one who died very young. Her life has been hard. Yet her joys have been many and she is always ready to give you a smile and a wonderful bear hug of love. She lights up a room through her enthusiasm for her children and grandchildren. For her 80th birthday, her children arranged for a surprise party that overwhelmed her with joy and happiness. The photos of the day still provide her immense happiness even as her own health has been precarious. She has moments of despair and unhappiness like the rest of us. But she also has a 'lift yourself up by the bootstraps' kind of attitude that will tolerate unhappiness for only so long. Then it is back to figuring out how she can help others.

It is not the events in our lives that determine how we talk to ourselves. It is not the hurts we have felt nor the love that we experience that determines what we say to ourselves. It is not just an attitude of the glass half full or half empty that makes us talk in a certain way.

We choose what we say to ourselves. We must now choose to listen more carefully to what we say and decide if we want to change our self-talk.

It is what we choose to say to ourselves that comes back to either harm us or provide us genuine moments of happiness, joy, gratitude, peacefulness and love. We choose whether our self-talk leads to moments of loneliness, fear and neglect or moments of connection, compassion and personal value.

You can make a concerted effort to listen to your conscious self-talk. Does what you say to yourself or others start with *Yes but....* when you are thinking of something or listening to someone's ideas? If you do, then you are likely not thinking about what someone has just said or an idea you have thought of. You are thinking instead of all the reasons that the idea is wrong or ill advized. You discount an opportunity to learn and be open to a different viewpoint. You miss an opportunity to be happier.

Catch yourself saying positive and encouraging self-talk and purposely choose to do it more often. Will you be happier for it? Of course.

Happiness and Sickness

One of my greatest fears is sickness. I have had other fears that I have overcome (e.g., a fear of public speaking and a fear of writing). I have other fears too but they are, frankly, less likely to happen, such as a fear of torture or being imprisoned. My line of work and where I live make it unlikely that I will ever be tortured or imprisoned.

However, most of us get seriously ill at some point. People often lose a sense of control when they are sick. People around them either do everything for them, including making all the decisions, or they stay away all together. Can you be happy and sick at the same time?

Well if you agree with anything I have said so far, then you might answer yes in your head but *I'm not so sure* in your stomach. That is how I answer the question too. I suppose what I am trying to do now is to see how I might be able to convince my stomach that it is all right to be sick and happy at the same time.

How would I feel if I found out that I had terminal cancer? How would I feel if I found out my wife, children or sister had a disease that could kill them? I spend more than the average amounts of time thinking about these questions. The nature of a lot of my public speaking in hospice care forces me to look at my fears more often than I would like sometimes.

I sometimes look at the questions and say that I would do all right if I would not have to involve other people and make them sad. Or I will look at the questions and think that I could handle the disease but not the tests and treatments for the disease. Sometimes I hope that all my loved ones die first so that they will not have to go through the suffering of my death. Before you think that is very nice of me to want to avoid other people having to suffer I must confess that I think it would be easier to face someone else's death than to watch them suffer through my dying. Very selfish actually.

So what do I do? I try to start by recognizing that everyone gets sick. Some people get well and some do not. Billions of people have been born on this earth and billions have died. I try to put my possible illness in that perspective. I am not the first person to experience illness and I am not the first person who has faced death. My fears are not reduced by this awareness because I have not faced my own serious illness yet. I know that I will need a substantial amount of control over my treatment and over how I will live until I die. I know that all but one of my illnesses will not kill me, therefore, I will need to plan things for after my illnesses to help me get through it. I know I will need to be needed and valued if I am very sick. I know I will need to be busy as much as possible. I know I will need to talk, listen, write, laugh, and cry. I know I will need happiness in my life and time to be unhappy and worry. I know that everything I think I will need and want may be different once I am sick.

What I know is that I need to work some of my fears out before I get sick or before other people close to me get sick. I know that even if I do not prepare that I will make it through. How do I know that?

I was 21 years old when I returned from doing volunteer work in Latin America. I was unprepared for the return culture shock I experienced. I felt out of control, immensely unhappy, sad, angry, obsessively worried, lonely and scared. Anxiety attacks were my constant companion. I tried to fill my time with teaching but during any free time, especially weekends, I thought I was going crazy.

My mother was sick at the time with angina. There were times when she was in terrible pain but she stoically accepted it and tried to live around it. There was a specific day when I thought that I could not handle living anymore. My mind and body (I had terrible stomach problems) seemed to exist outside of me, outside of my control. My mother was resting in bed on this day and I went to her in a panic. I said I thought I was going crazy. I asked her what I should do and whether or not she thought I would make it.

She gave the answer you would expect from a mother—that things would turn out okay in time. I asked her how she knew. I will never forget her answer. It was powerful beyond words. She had been physically abused as a child, had lived through the German occupation of her town, had seen her father's business and family home crumble before her eyes as the bombs dropped, she had seen her boyfriend go off to fight in Indonesia from 1947-49 (my dad), she had immigrated to Canada without speaking a word of English, she was a feminist before the word was popular, and she had raised two children while knowing that she would not live a long time (she died when she was 53). All of those experiences came through her powerful, compassionate brown eyes. When I asked her how she knew I would be okay she said, "*I know*" with such quiet conviction that I believed her instantly. It was a simple answer to a complex question and I believed her. She knew what it was to suffer. She knew from personal experience that if she could survive, so could I. She knew from personal experience that if she could find happiness, so could I. From then on I knew I would be okay. It took nearly 2 years but I became okay again. Ironically it was just in time to help her before she died.

How do I know I will survive all but one illness even though I am terribly afraid of them? I just do.

Happiness and Suicide

I have spent time with people who have wanted to die. Some wanted to die because they were already dying of a terminal illness. Others wanted to die because they saw no hope in their daily life or future. I was most helpful when I did not argue with them about why their decision was wrong. I tried to listen to their worries and anxieties, their hopes and dreams and their reasoning.

Some were close (within hours) of acting on their decision to die. Some based their decision on what many would consider a rational, logical sequence of beliefs. Given similar circumstances, many of us would have come up with similar conclusions.

In each case, the person decided not to go ahead. For some it was a religious fear of going to hell. For most it was that living one more day of their life seemed the better option than an eternity of uncertainty. For others it was because they recognized and felt that people still needed them to be a parent, friend, sibling or child. They still had things to do.

I once asked a friend of mine who has spent most of his adult life in one institution or another (because he has a mild developmental disability) whether he was ever suicidal. He had gone through over 20 years of life in a mental institution including some shock treatments, the removal of all of his personal property (easier to keep track that way), the loss of all of his teeth (don't have to brush them then) and much more. He was isolated from his family since the institution was not in the city where his family lived. He was placed in the institution because the parents were convinced by well-meaning professionals that it would be best for him and for them.

So given all of this history I asked him one day if he had ever been suicidal. He is twenty years older than me and looked at me like I was a stupid child. *Harry, I'm not crazy you know!* His life has been anything but wonderful for him but it was still worth living. I gave him a lot of credit for his insights into what makes life worth living. Many of them were similar to what Viktor Frankl mentions at the beginning of this book—and yet, my friend is the one labelled intellectually disabled!

I asked a physician who has many patients with ALS (Lou Gerhig's Disease) if any of his more than 200 patients were suicidal. He said that some were when they first came to him. They wanted a sense of control over their lives that an acceptance of suicide gave them. If they always had an 'out' they could tolerate so much more. Some of the patients said that they wanted to live until they needed to go onto a respirator. They didn't want to live with one of those. Until, that is, it came time to decide whether they would go on a respirator or not.

All of them chose the respirator because they had a child's wedding to attend, a granddaughter's baptism to witness, a bit more tidying up of their affairs to do. Each of his patients, however, never feared that talking about suicidal thoughts would cause the doctor to turn away or diagnose them as 'depressed' and force medication on them.

In my case, the roller coaster ride of helping people through suicidal times reinforces this idea for me. Any of these people may have chosen to die and I would not have physically stopped them. Some decisions must be left to the people themselves. However, I did not want them to make such a decision without someone nearby who loved them and who would listen to their stories. I did not prevent any suicides. I gave people a sympathetic ear and time to think out loud some of what most worried them.

Would I have 'failed' them, if they had chosen death. No, I don't think so. Would I have failed them if I had turned away because it was too painful to help? Yes, I think so. Isolation and a lack of compassionate people around you, I believe, is one of the greatest reasons why people want to die–not the only reason, mind you–but one of the greatest.

Should I have forced them to seek psychiatric help against their will? Not in these cases. There are people who need that kind of support, but these people were not in that category. Several were already under a psychiatrist's care and forced treatment in a locked ward would only have made things worse.

Why, then, do seemingly okay people with loving families and friends around them, want to die? I am not a therapist or mental health expert. I have been a friend and what I have learned is this–in the end, all human decisions are based on perceptions (some that are clearly inaccurate to other people but not to the person who holds them). Given certain perceptions, logical conclusions are drawn in their minds that are usually combined with sleeplessness, over use of medications, alcohol or drugs, that lead to thoughts of suicide, an attempted suicide or an actual suicide. If someone is there to notice the changes in a person's personality, their sleep habits, their giving away all their possessions and similar 'clues', then that person may be helped and they may not die. Sadly, it doesn't always work out that way.

Is there room for happiness in any of this? Of course there is. With the people I have mentioned, there were still moments of laughter, off-color death humor, and stories told and retold. Some felt some relief that someone would listen without telling them what to do. They were allowed the freedom to express their thoughts and feelings without a time limit. In all these cases, humor, laughter, and reflection on moments of past happiness led to new 'happy' memories for us. These moments were not enough, in themselves, to convince someone that suicide was not right for them— but they helped. They helped them and they helped me. They passed time so there was more opportunity to reflect on alternatives.

I am grateful for these opportunities to be there with those struggling with the most fundamental question on the meaning of life. I do not wish this situation on anyone as it is a painful one in many ways, but it is also life affirming–it refocuses my own perceptions of why life is worth living. It helps me reaffirm my love for so many wonderful people in my life. It allows me time to slow down enough (one can't hurry these kinds of discussions) to examine my own beliefs and values. It allowed me time for one more hug, one more laugh and one more shared tear of friendship together.

Happiness and War/Hate

I had a friend who was 86 years old. I sometimes asked her difficult questions to learn from her wisdom. We had different religious beliefs, she and I, but we shared a love of God, a love of others and we both worked at loving ourselves better.

I asked her one day what she thought of war. Her answer was immediate and powerful. OH I DON'T WAR, CHILD. I had never heard it put more clearly than that. *I don't war.* In the English language, the word war is a noun, a thing. We make war or we declare war. What my friend did was use the word as a verb, an action. She did not war. Her idea was a simple one; a profound one. Yet, a difficult idea to follow into action.

I mentioned that I thought, as do many others, that the opposite of love is not hate but fear. If that is true then hate and wars are results of fear. What is it we fear that allows us to hate millions of people and fight a war. On a trip to Europe I did a lot of bicycling with my aunt. We rode over 250 miles in two weeks and it was wonderful. One day we rode by a war cemetery. There are more than a few of them in The Netherlands. This was a German war cemetery. The gate to get in was deceiving as most of the cemeteries are relatively small and extremely well kept by the Dutch people. This cemetery was also very well kept. It was, however, huge. There were 31,585 soldiers buried in that cemetery. They had all died in the final months of the war. They were young men, mostly drafted, to fight a war I doubt they understood or supported. They would have much preferred to be home with their families and sweethearts than in the muddy fields of Holland that spring, 1944.

When I stood in the middle of that cemetery I could see graves as far as the eye could see in all directions. To say I felt sadness and anger at the wastefulness does not begin to tell the story.

Years before that I had visited Dachau with my father and sister. I had only seen pictures of concentration camps. The feelings I felt walking under the entrance seen by millions of people in photos and film were powerful and sad. There was a monument there built in memory of the people who had died in the camp. The monument had a large sign which read, *Never Again*. I was so angry when I read it. Angry because it implied that the killing and suffering had stopped. It has not. There are people throughout the world today who suffer for political, economic or religious reasons. There is the constant warfare somewhere in the world, often in more places than one. We are no more humane today as a species than we were in World War II. We have never stopped killing, torturing, raping and slaughtering our fellow human beings. We have only moved the location and limited, so far, the fighting to smaller regions. We have never learned the lessons of history.

How then can I think of war and hate in the same breath as happiness. Just these few examples above show you some of the horror that exists in the name of democracy and freedom. Twenty million people died in World War II–20,000,000.

When I asked my parents and grandfather about the war I was surprised to hear that they still went dancing on a Saturday night or out for a date by the river. People still had children and farmed their lands. Companies still worked and taxes were still paid. Their government was run by Germans and their town was occupied by both the English and the Germans at different times. They knew that many of the soldiers were just young boys originally keen on adventure but quickly homesick for their families and girlfriends. They talked to these soldiers while my Dad also helped smuggle people out of

Germany. For him it was an adventure as a young farm boy who knew the back woods of their border town with Germany so well. No special ideology here. Young men and women who lived through five years of uncertainty; both the uncertainty of war but also the uncertainty of growing into adults.

There was happiness and fear together. Families still celebrated holidays and special days. People still had parties and went to church. People who tended to be happy by nature continued that way. People who tended to be unhappy continued that way too.

What is the modern lesson about war, hatred and happiness? It is the same as what I said about poverty and happiness, I think. We do not have to be unhappy, angry or overwhelmed by war and hatred to make changes. People can remain happy or become happier and have the extra energy it takes to prevent more torture, hatred and war.

Happiness can be a measuring stick against which people can see how stupid war is. Those

31,585 soldiers in the cemetery in the town of Ysselsteyn will never be happy again on this earth. That was taken from them. Did we need to rob the happiness of the women and men in the Persian Gulf to protect oil fields? Did Holland really need to send thousands of soldiers, including my father, to Indonesia to fight a losing battle for independence just so that the rich Dutch corporations could get their assets out of the country? Did we have to have over 50,000 North American soldiers die in Viet Nam to prevent the communists from ruling the world? Did the 50,000 men who died in 3 days of hand-to-hand fighting in Gettysburg during the American Civil War need to die to determine whether the North or the South should win?

The end of the 1980s helped us answer those questions. Historic changes in Europe have proven that revolutions do not have to involve the deaths of millions of people. When the Berlin Wall collapsed and the Iron Curtain was removed without bloodshed, we saw dramatic change without violence. Yes there are economic prices to pay and people will be inconvenienced by all these changes. Might some of these changes have happened sooner if twenty million had not died in World War II? What would have happened if there was a much greater peaceful resistance against Hitler? There would still have been people murdered. There would still have been violence and strife. But would as many sons and daughters, husbands and wives and parents have died?

Would less people have suffered and died (a utilitarian view)? Would Russia and the United States not have become so powerful and extended a cold war with the enormous cost of nuclear and other arms build up? Why are these questions not answered before we allow our leaders to send yet another generation of children to war.

I used to be a stronger supporter of using force to defend freedom. I am becoming more interested in knowing how peaceful resistance toward deadly military aggression could change our history. Are the lessons of Eastern Europe important enough to show us that no leader or leaders can hold their populations in fear and degradation for ever?

In Holland, during World War II, the SS visited a hospital to demand that the doctors and administrators release the name of any disabled or mentally ill patients. The doctors and administrators did not know what would be done with their patients but they could guess. They might not have guessed the extent of the Nazi death camps, but they had heard rumors. So they refused to prepare such a list for the SS. They were warned that if they refused, some of them would be killed. These brave and stubborn doctors and administrators refused none the less and a few were, in fact, killed. The SS could easily have gone room to room to find the patients they were looking for but they wanted compliance. When they did not get it, they left the hospital and the rest of the doctors and administrators alone and the patients were safe.

Yes, some people died in this example—some very highly valued men who could easily have taken a different route. Their non-violence, however, led to many more being saved. What can we learn from this? What did we learn from the non-violence of Mahatma Ghandi in India or Martin Luther King Jr. in the United States or Nelson Mandela for most of his life in South Africa or resistance in the Eastern communist countries?

Non-violence may, or may not, take longer than violent war but the deaths are measurably fewer. If we tried this at a state and international level, rather than at the individual level, would we be able to prevent evil dictators from mass genocide without having to kill even more people to stop them? I think so. I hope we try in my life time.

I would like to think that one day I will have more answers to these questions for myself. For now I would like to be supportive of the individual soldiers who fight our leaders' battles while, at the same time borrowing from my friend's words that *I don't war*. This takes some real changing in thinking for me but I think it will work. What do our leaders fear so much that they want us to hate other world leaders and declare war against them? How much of their fear is economically driven? How much of the fear has to do with getting elected? Why are there so many companies making a fortune from wars? Do they help start wars so that they can continue to make money? After all, where do these non-democratic leaders who want to take over the world get their weapons? I hope to understand this better and to use happiness and fear as yardsticks for why we and our leaders allow this stupidity, this deadly stupidity, to go on.

The Rules of Being Happier More Often

(Further Conclusions)

If you finish this book by saying: *Well this was pretty basic stuff. Anyone could have written this.* BRAVO!

Anyone could write this stuff because it is simple to understand, if not always easy to do. The usefulness of this book, however, will come out of asking yourself, *Do I practice these basics? If so which ones? Which don't I practice and what stops me from doing what I believe is best for me?* Which of these ideas in this long letter make sense to me; which do not? Why?

How would you write this book differently? Why?

What are your stories that go with each topic? How could you help other people and yourself through your stories and those of people you know? Use this letter as an excuse to do some thinking, talking and writing for yourself and to others.

Your have basically three choices now:

1. choose to do nothing different for now and live life as it comes—your time to try different things may not be now,
2. choose to be happier more often,
3. choose to find other answers (and questions).

Enjoy whichever choice you make.

If you remember one thing from this letter I hope it is to compare yourself to Viktor Frankl's life experiences. No matter the fragility of your life, your vulnerability to external forces that can, at any time, take away your joy and happiness, there will be moments of happiness. Whether it is like the person who walks through the concentration camp offering comfort or a last piece of bread or the person who shares a memory of their wife who has already died in the gas chambers, these are treasures that can occur during weeks, months and years of despair. Most of us do not have to experience such deprivation, humiliation and isolation—however, it is somewhat comforting to know that moments of happiness can exist in such times and, therefore, during our own trials and tribulations. It is being open to such moments of happiness, peacefulness, joy, calmness and excitement that makes life worth sharing with others.

I'd like to leave you with several memory aids that might help you put some of the information in this book/letter into context for your own situations. I hope they might help you design your own 'rules' or summaries so that you experience more moments of happiness in your life.

Other Ways to Summarize Being Happier More Often

There are so many memory aids to help you practice some of what we have looked at together in this book. Here are a few:

YOUR 10 RULES FOR BEING HAPPIER MORE OFTEN (AND SUCCESSFUL!)

This repeats the rules from earlier in the book. We will go from 10 down to number 1. Each rule is important in its own way so don't sneak ahead in the list. Each rule will help you choose to be happier more often starting today.

10. SMILE and laugh more often. A 10-minute belly laugh massages your internal organs better than hours of quiet meditation.

9. BREATHE slowly and deeply at least 3 times a day for 5-10 minutes. You can do this while you are working at your desk, driving your car, walking your dog, waiting in a line, etc.

8. MUSIC – listen, sing, write, or dance. Use energizing or relaxing music, depending on how you would like to be happy at that moment.

7. RELATIONSHIPS – nurture the ones you have; create new ones with people older and younger. If you work 10-12 hour days and say you are doing it for your family, you are kidding yourself. Absence does not make the heart grow founder if you are absent most of every day of your working life. Go home and nurture your family and friends.

6. EMOTIONAL JOY – find out what makes you smile, laugh, and feel peaceful and write down your favorite 10. Then do them more often. It could be watching your child sleep, sitting quietly on a park bench, watching a favorite comedy on TV, going for lunch or a walk with a dear friend you rarely see, shar-

ing a family meal together more often, holding hands with your sweetie, eating some of Mom's homemade cookies or working with your Dad on a project. Whatever works for you, do it more often. Don't wait for retirement or for when you have more time.

5. INTELLECTUAL INTERESTS – knowledge is power and power gives one a sense of confidence and happiness. Find out about what you need to know to live a good life, as you define it. Learn about managing your finances instead of letting money manage you. Find out about what you need to do to stay healthy. How will you provide care to your parents, spouse, children, friends, neighbors? Learn these things as you need them and teach others when they need the same knowledge and skills. *Always look for the wonder in learning and teach what you learn to others. Inspire others through your experiences.*

4. PHYSICALLY move around to release natural endorphins that make you feel good and to act as distractions. Even if you are stuck in

one place, find ways to move your body and at your earliest chance, move it in a different place (e.g., home, forest, beach, playground) to benefit from the change of scene as well.

3. PRACTICE A LIFE-AFFIRMING BELIEF beyond yourself. Whether through religion, a more general spirituality or a love of nature, go beyond yourself so you have something to hold on to when you need that strength, courage, and persistence. Belief only in yourself or your family and friends may mean you do not have the resources to struggle through really difficult times nor the comfort of feeling part of something bigger and better.

2. APPLY ANCIENT WISDOM – We are not alone. We are not the first people to try and figure out the meaning of life or how to live a good life. Learn what other people have concluded after lifetimes of study and experiences. We have so much more in common with people of different cultures and from different centuries.

1. HAPPIERMOREOFTEN NOW — Put the other 9 rules to work starting now. Return to them often. Go to our website for further ideas, tips, reports on studies and to share your experiences with others. When you reverse the order of the rules above you will get a HAPPIER MBS. This is a tongue-in-cheek way of saying there is so much BS in the world, find the true gems of how to enjoy your life everyday; more often, than you do now. When you do, you will be happier more often and have earned a *Masters in Being Successful* (MBS)! Congratulations!

H appier more often

A pply ancient wisdom

P ractice a life-affirming belief

P hysically move

I ntellectual interests

E motional joy

R elationships – nurture and create new ones

M usic

B reathe slowly and deeply

S mile and laugh more often!

There are so many ways of defining how to live your life. It is important that you create your own list based on the wisdom of others and what you know works for you.

Ancient Wisdom

There is no single right way to choose to be happier. Recognizing happiness as a choice will get you started!

Here are some ancient wisdoms that may also help you:

WISDOM #1: Relationships are more important than good health, great vacations, lots of money or prestige.

WISDOM #2: Words that divide us, harm us. There is no *us* and *them* — only us. We are all members of the human family and we cannot, nor should not, be divided by how we look or act or by what we achieve in life.

WISDOM #3: Love and happiness, like fear and hatred, are choices we make. Don't let someone else tell you how to feel or how to live your life if these ways are harmful to others.

WISDOM #4: Concentrate on doing what is possible and doing that in positive ways. Do not concentrate on what is not possible as this drains your energy to do much of anything good in your life.

WISDOM #5: Learn from others who have spent their lives examining wisdom and how it applies to our daily living.

THE HAPPINESS POSTER

Create your own poster defining happiness for you. Here is my sample.

H ealthy balance of meeting
my physical, emotional,
spiritual and information
needs

A ttitude that says I can find
ways to increase my hap-
piness every day

P hilosophy of life that
looks for wonder, peace,
joy, love, calmness and
happiness on how to do
good for goodness sake

P ersonal commitment to
improve my capacity to
laugh, love and learn

I ntellectual commitment
to continue my life-long
learning

N urture all the important
relationships in my life as
nothing else really mat-
ters

E njoy more of life's simple
pleasures—a bit more
each day

S piritually acknowledge a
greater good, a higher
order of things

S ucceed in this quest as I
have never succeeded
before!

How to Apply Happiness in the Workplace and at Home: Rules to Lead By

I use the following rules in teaching management and leadership development to front-line and senior managers. They really work!

1. Say *Hello* to everyone who looks at you.
2. Do not listen to or encourage gossip. It is usually wrong anyway.
3. Do not let someone vent or complain about something more than once. If they want to work to resolve the situation; help them. If they just want to complain; ignore them and

tell them clearly you do not want to hear the complaint again.

4. If you do not tell someone they are doing something that angers or annoys you, you can't blame them if they do it again.

5. Do not listen to racist, sexist humor. Discourage others from using it.

6. Discipline means *to follow* rather than *to punish*. So lead by example and through instruction.

7. Use appropriate humor, laughter and playfulness to help make as many days memorable and energizing as possible.

8. Be clear with expectations and praise–never begin a critique with a compliment. End some critiques with a compliment. That way, all compliments are accepted for what they are rather than a preamble to a list of problems or faults.

9. People only hear or read 20% of what you are communicating and forget 80% of that within 24 hours. If you want them to remember something, communicate it more

than once and in various ways. You are 100% responsible for effective communications. It would be nice if everyone took full responsibility for effective communications but it does not usually work that way. If it is important to you, you must take 100% responsibility.

10. Someone has to begin the conflict resolution process—it is not fair that it is often you, but if the conflict is important enough, be first.

~

Okay, just one more. This is addictive you know. As you can see, we could keep at this forever. There are so many rules for effective living.

ONE MORE LIST

For those of you who like lists, here is a last one of things you can do to find more happiness every day:

- Nurture your family and friend relationships more often.
- Nurture your sense of community more often. Meet your neighbors. Help them out. Learn from them.
- Nurture your spirituality.
- Nurture a gratitude attitude.
- Learn to relax your body's muscles and your mind. Meditate, pray, learn deep relaxation techniques.
- Get enough sleep and exercise and eat well more often than not.
- Do your best at work and at play. Don't just get by – get high on accomplishing new tasks and goals.
- Fake it till you make it. Pretending to be happy more often may actually lead your mind (which doesn't distinguish reality from imagination) to release those wonderful

mind chemicals that makes you feel more happy.

- Forgive more. Say please and thank you more.
- Smile more.
- Breathe deeply and slowly more often.
- Recognize that money doesn't make happiness but a middle class income takes away some stresses.
- Get used to being silent and turning off the TV, stereo and other noise makers.
- Find a balance between love, gratitude and service. Find ways to go out of your way to help others. Make a difference in the lives of others and be grateful for all the help you receive.
- Slow down your life. Cut out some of the distractions that keep you from living. For example, too much TV, reading, sports and such prevents you from actually talking and being with people.
- Savor your food and drink. Slow down how quickly you eat. Eat without doing anything

else like watching TV. Concentrate on the food and the company.

- Try to eat at least one meal a day with your family. Family meals are a main determiner of successful children (success in school, socializing and life in general).

- Ask for and give more hugs, cuddles and hand holding.

- Laugh more often. You can even begin laughing just for the fun of it. You don't actually need a reason to laugh. Just start. If you are with other people they will join in and then you have a reason to laugh together.

Begin now by writing your own list of top 10 rules then put them somewhere you can see them everyday. If you are not happy more often than you are now, go back to your list. This process is GUARANTEED to help you feel happier more often. It is an easy guarantee to make, because you control the results!

∼

So the letter is over. I have enjoyed writing and rewriting this for you and hope that some of it is helpful to you.

May you find more happiness each day and may you share it with others. May you find simpler responses to complex situations. May you concentrate on what is possible in positive ways rather than concentrate on the impossible in energy-draining ways. May you share this book with others and compare notes so that we can all live fully until we die.

Gratefully and Happily yours (more often than I used to be anyway!),

Your friend,

HARRY

Recognize that you already know what to do—now just commit to doing it!

Choose to be happier more often and help others do the same.

References

The following references are only a few of the many excellent resources that you can find in your local libraries and book stores. You can also look for journal articles, magazine reports, films, videos and audio cassettes. Keep in mind how much you can learn from the people you know. Talk to older and younger people.

Also remember that your greatest expert is yourself....write a journal, look at yourself when you are happy and sad and find out why.

Brashich, Audrey D. (2006). *All made up*. New York: Walker and Company
A former beauty magazine editor and model, Brashich tells young girls and teenagers about how corporations define beauty and then make extraordinary profits selling beauty products and services. The

emphasis should be, according to Brashich, on women of distinction rather than women with short-lived modelling careers.

Cousins, Norman. (1979). *Anatomy of an illness as perceived by the patient.* New York: W. W. Norton.

How this magazine editor overcame the traumas of a terminal illness using humor, laughter, old comedy films, while also taking personal control over his overall treatment and health. Includes interviews of Pablo Cassals and Albert Schweitzer.

Frankl, Viktor E. (1984). *Man's search for meaning* (revised and updated). New York: Washington Square Press.

Story of the internationally known psychiatrist, Viktor Frankl's survival in Nazi concentration camps and his conclusion that our primary motivational force is our search for meaning.

Fulghum, Robert. (1986). *All I really need to know I learned in kindergarten.* New York: Villard Books (Random House).

Fulghum has had many different careers in his lifetime yet summarizes the main lessons of his life based on the simple principles learned in kindergarten.

Fynn. (1974). *Mister God this is Anna*. London: William Collins & Sons.

Story of a young girl in East End London whose search for meaning, truth, beauty and goodness is aided by her friendship with Mister God. A timeless book of wonder about a young genius who lives a complete life in a few short years.

Levit, Rose. (1974). *Ellen: A short life long remembered*. New York: Bantam Books.

A mother's story of the illness and death of her teenage daughter. It brings in the added emotions of her own divorce and the ex-husband's love for his daughter plus the love and tensions between Ellen and her older sister.

Miller, Merle. (1973, 1974). *Plain speaking: An oral biography of Harry S. Truman*. New York: Berkley Publishing Company.

A transcription of conversations between the former U.S. President and Miller examining many aspects of human nature and politics as experienced by the failed businessman from Independence Missouri who rose to become president, much to many people's surprise.

O'Kelly, Eugene with Andrew Postman. (2006). *Chasing Daylight: How My Forthcoming Death Transformed My Life*. New York: McGraw-Hill. Last chapter by his wife, after his death.

An autobiography by the Chair of KPMG Accounting firm in the U.S. of his last 3 months of life. Insightful in his examination of what is truly important in life (relationships with loved ones) and how that can be balanced with a busy work life.

Popkin, Richard H. and Stroll, Avrum. (1956). *Philosophy made simple*. New York: Doubleday. An excellent overview of philosophy by two University of California philosophy professors. They write in fairly clear language and give information on such topics as ethics, methaphysics, and the philosophies of politics, religion, logic and modern philosophy.

Unger, Jim. (1982). *Herman: For the hospitalized*. Kansas City: Universal Press Syndicate.

Only one sample among hundreds of the humor and enjoyment we can get from the unique perspective of life found in cartoons.

Acknowledgements

I have been very fortunate in my life to have many family members and friends share their ideas, beliefs and stories with me so I could learn from them as much as I learned through my own life experiences.

Naturally MY PARENTS were my greatest early teachers. They experienced war (World War II living in Holland just over the border from Germany), as a soldier for my father (Dutch army in Indonesia from 1947-1949), the poverty of those war years, immigrating to Canada with two young children and so much more. To say I am grateful for all they taught me does not begin to repay their countless gifts to me. I can only hope that my children feel as loved, supported, encouraged and comforted as I did for the years we were together.

My good fortune continued of meeting and marrying my best friend and kindred spirit, JANET KLEES. To get to know a woman as a friend first and girlfriend later on is a wonderful opportunity. We could concentrate on getting to know each other personally without the baggage of first dates, intimacy expectations, etc. I highly recommend this route!

When you have lived for more than 50 years, there are hundreds of other people who have helped you become who you are. Some of them teach you what you need to learn. Others teach you, through their examples, of what not to do. Each provides an opportunity of acquiring or recognizing ancient wisdom that can help you live more happily.

Included in this large group for me are my many family members, friends over the years, their families, my teachers, employers, work colleagues, neighbors, and media/cultural folks (e.g., writers, actors, musicians, artists, scientists, historians, adventures, explorers, photographers). Each leaves a mark—some conscious and many unconscious. I am grateful to them all!

Specifically, I am grateful to DIANA POTTS for reminding me that my long letter to family and friends for Christmas in 1990 helped her. She encouraged me to look at the letter again, revise it and publish it more widely. STONEY KUDEL provided insights and revisions that have made the book better. RICK SPENCE, an exceptional business journalist and editor, has known about many of my other publications and said, *Finally something happy!* referring to my joy in writing books to help people who are dying and their families.

DIANE HUSON has provided support and encouragement and revisions for this book and many others. Her friendship over the past 27 years is invaluable and I am genuinely grateful.

My newest teachers are my children BRAM and JOANNA. Through each of their life phases I learn so much from and about them. I am fortunate to be able to spend many more of my daily hours with them than most parents. Not only do I do most of my work at home, my wife and I have also home schooled our children. To see them learn with such gusto, self-direction and joy is truly life affirming and a blessing. Thank you Joanna and Bram for teaching me so much about life and living and doing it with more happiness than I might otherwise.

About the Author

HARRY VAN BOMMEL is the author of over 35 books. He speaks and gives workshops internationally about his many areas of interest. He has a Masters Degree in Adult Education but most of his learning has been self-directed. He is a founder of several organizations including:

- BIOGRAPHERS INTERNATIONAL ORGANIZATION: BIO, a body to support independent and academic biographers around the world to share resources and skills for their mutual benefit.

- CANADA 150, a project to encourage Canadians to record their life and community histories in time for Canada's 150th birthday in 2017 (http://www.canada150.com).

- The CANADIAN HOSPICE PALLIATIVE CARE ASSOCIATION: a national body supporting the work of professionals and volunteers in this field (http://www.chpca.net).

- The HOSPICE ASSOCIATION OF ONTARIO: a provincial body concentrating on supporting community-based hospice palliative care (http://www.hospice.on.ca)
- RESOURCES SUPPORTING FAMILY AND COMMUNITY LEGACIES INC., an international non-profit organization that provides online resources as well as eBooks and paperback books in the fields of caregiving, home and hospice care, community development, learning and helping people record their life and family stories.

  (http://www.legacies.ca)
- NAVCARE, a national project to help patients and families navigate whatever health care systems exist in their communities using online resources, books, training programs and the use of Health Care advisors (http://www.navCare.org).
- PSD CONSULTANTS for the professional and personal development of workers, managers

and leaders in such fields as health care, industry, manufacturing, government, education, social services and non-profit organizations.

(http://www.psd-consultants.com)

A great deal of his understanding of happiness comes through his experiences of helping his parents and grandfather to live at home until they died. He has experienced many of the 'downs' of life including a business failure early in his career. He has also experienced many of the 'highs' including finding and marrying his kindred spirit, having two wonderful children and very good friends. His work in hospice palliative care, caregiving, management and staff development, helping people record their life stories and much more keep him grounded to what is important in life. Interviewing people at the end of their lives reminds him constantly that nurturing relationships is the key to any happy and successful life.

Mr. van Bommel's books can be found at: http://www.legacies.ca where you can read them and/or buy either the electronic version or paperback editions for yourself and to give as gifts to your family and friends. More background information about him can be found at: www.harryvanbommel.com.

Mr. van Bommel can also be reached through writing to him at: harry@legacies.ca.

Check out http://www.happiermoreoften.com for more information, updated studies and special events related to this book.